THERE'S SOMETHING MAGICAL ABOUT
a BIG NEW SHINY idea

Hey there!

Easily distracted? No... not us! We're just open to inspiration! (RIGHT?)

And sure. Sometimes that "inspo" takes us on unexpected journeys with unexpected consequences. But that's part of the fun!
Right?

Except... when it isn't.
Except when our BIG NEW SHINY idea takes us into a BIG MESS that took us off track.

We can't just ignore all of our BIG NEW SHINY ideas. We just need to check them out a little before we leap into action

We need to decide: Will this be the idea people will rave about for generations to come? Or was it destined to live on only in this book, pure for the eyes of me alone?

This book is your record of BIG SHINY NEW ideas

It's your place to pop those idea interruptions, the drives to deep dive, the desires to follow your nose, that app that could resolve all the crap and all those amazing, energising and incredible thinks your brain is creating all the time

Here's to making some of them become a reality.

Rachel Klaver
Expert in falling down the BIG SHINY NEW idea
rabbit hole on a daily basis!

HOW TO USE this journal

1. Jot down your idea. You can use words, draw it out, or use a mixture of both. If it's an app, make sure you add the link to check out later.

2. Have a regular weekly "Let's check on my big shiny new ideas" time every week. Take a slower, more thoughtful look. Does it fit your goals? Will it make life easier or better? Do you have the budget to make it happen? Or the time? Will it distract you from another goal in a good way, or a bad way?

3. From there make a decision on whether it's a NOW, a SOON, or a LATER idea to implement. (Or perhaps make the call it's a NEVER)

4. Write down any steps, resources, or blocks you might need to sort out before you can make it happen.

TAKING ACTION

Look at areas such as cost, capacity, timelines, what equipment or people are required, and skill levels.

5. When you've actioned it, mark it off.

6. Come back to your BIG SHINY IDEA idea in a chosen timeframe (one month, three, six months, or more) and record the impact taking action had for you. This can help you evaluate if you should do more of this type of activity. You could also note anything you learned here too, so next time it works better.

> (If you're a visual person I have given you a "filled out" example of how this all works at the back of this journal. I sometimes need to see someone else's work to get started!)

MY "BIG SHINY NEW IDEA" PLAN

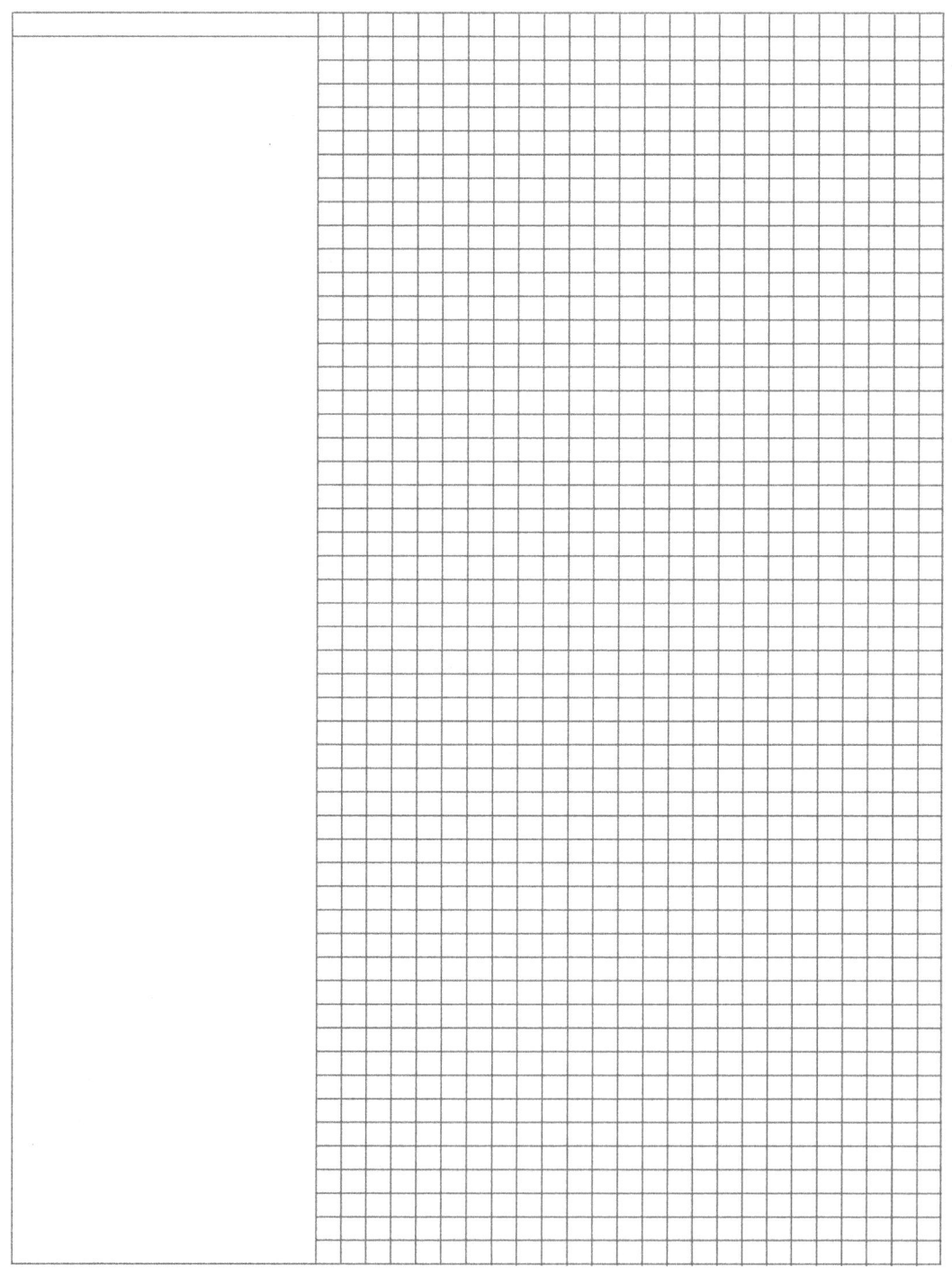

MY "BIG SHINY NEW" IDEA

My idea
....
....
....
....
....

Shine bright my idea. Shine bright.

SENSE CHECK:

- ☐ Helps with long-term plans
- ☐ Have the capacity to act
- ☐ Have the budget to act
- ☐ Have the skills required

What will make this idea shine?

POTENTIAL IMPACT
1 2 3 4 5 6 7 8 9 10

TIMELINE
NOW   SOON
LATER   NEVER

POTENTIAL BENEFITS   POTENTIAL DRAWBACKS

ACTIONED:

IMPACT:

MY "BIG SHINY NEW IDEA" PLAN

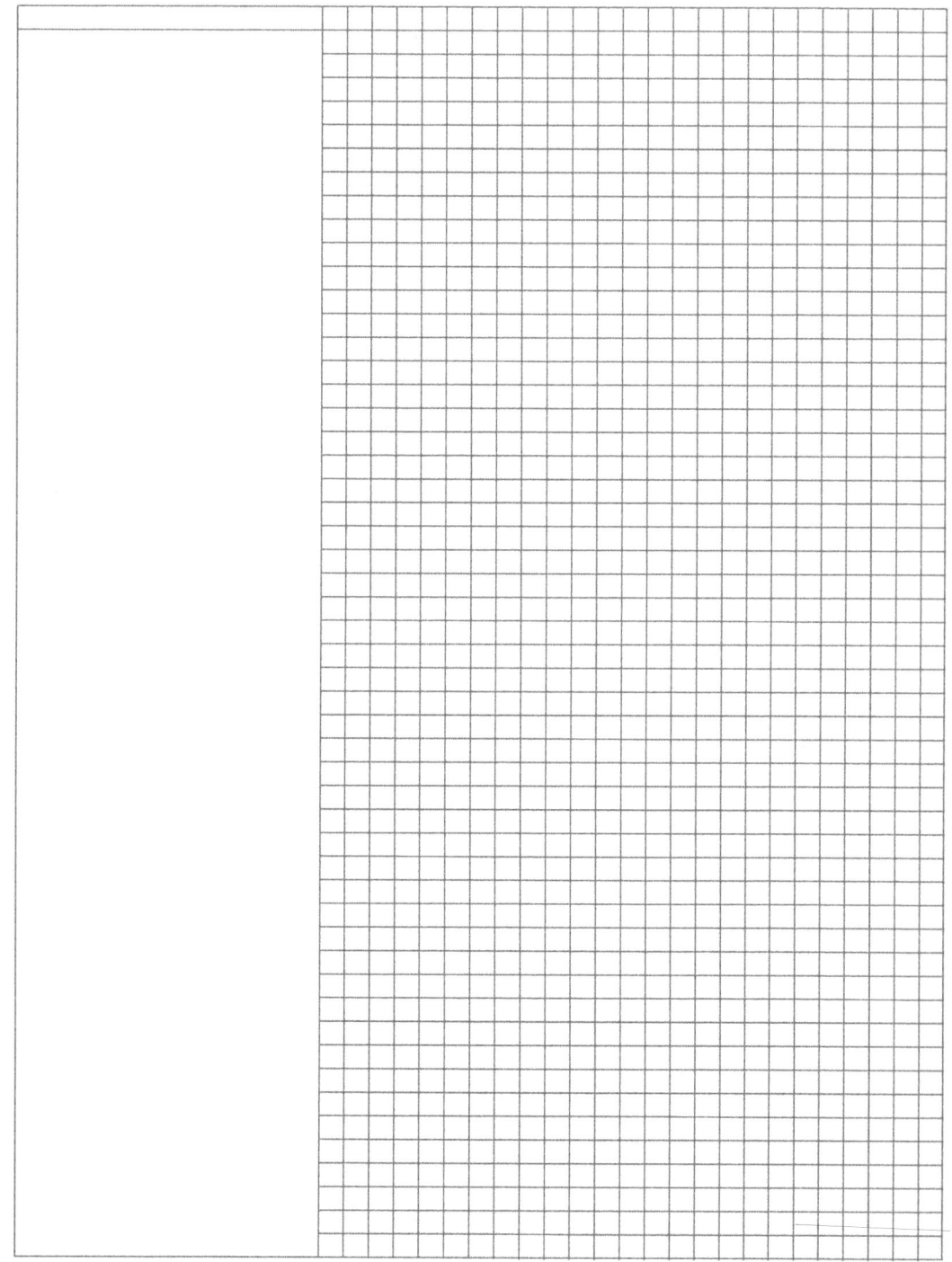

MY "BIG SHINY NEW" IDEA

My idea

....

....

....

....

....

....

Shine bright my idea. Shine bright.

SENSE CHECK:

☐ Helps with long-term plans

☐ Have the capacity to act

☐ Have the budget to act

☐ Have the skills required

What will make this idea shine?

POTENTIAL IMPACT
1 2 3 4 5 6 7 8 9 10

TIMELINE
NOW   SOON
LATER   NEVER

POTENTIAL BENEFITS   POTENTIAL DRAWBACKS

ACTIONED:

IMPACT:

MY "BIG SHINY NEW IDEA" PLAN

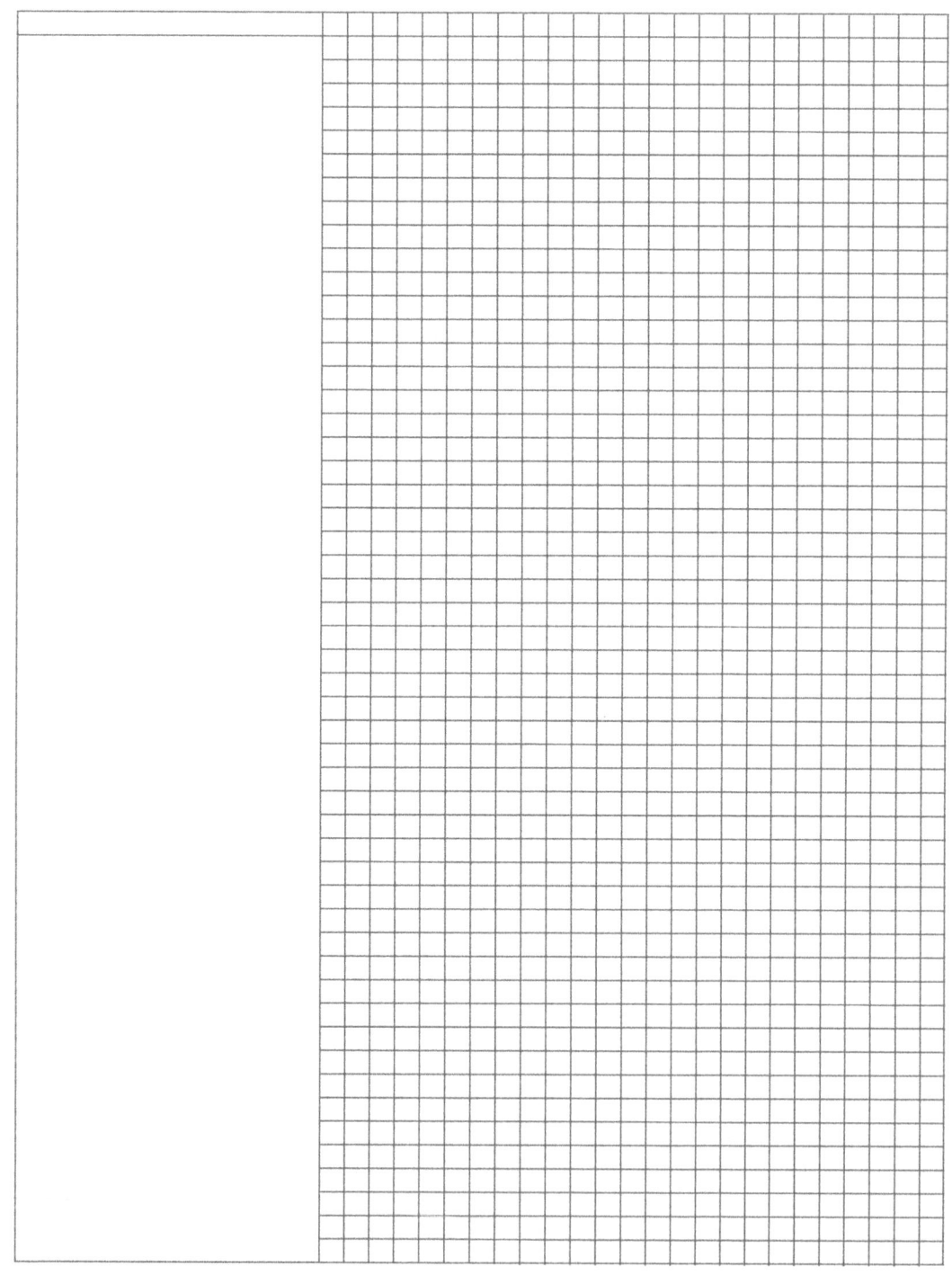

MY "BIG SHINY NEW" IDEA

My idea

....

....

....

....

....

....

Shine bright my idea. Shine bright.

SENSE CHECK:

☐ Helps with long-term plans

☐ Have the capacity to act

☐ Have the budget to act

☐ Have the skills required

What will make this idea shine?

POTENTIAL IMPACT
1 2 3 4 5 6 7 8 9 10

TIMELINE
NOW   SOON
LATER   NEVER

POTENTIAL BENEFITS   POTENTIAL DRAWBACKS

ACTIONED:

IMPACT:

MY "BIG SHINY NEW IDEA" PLAN

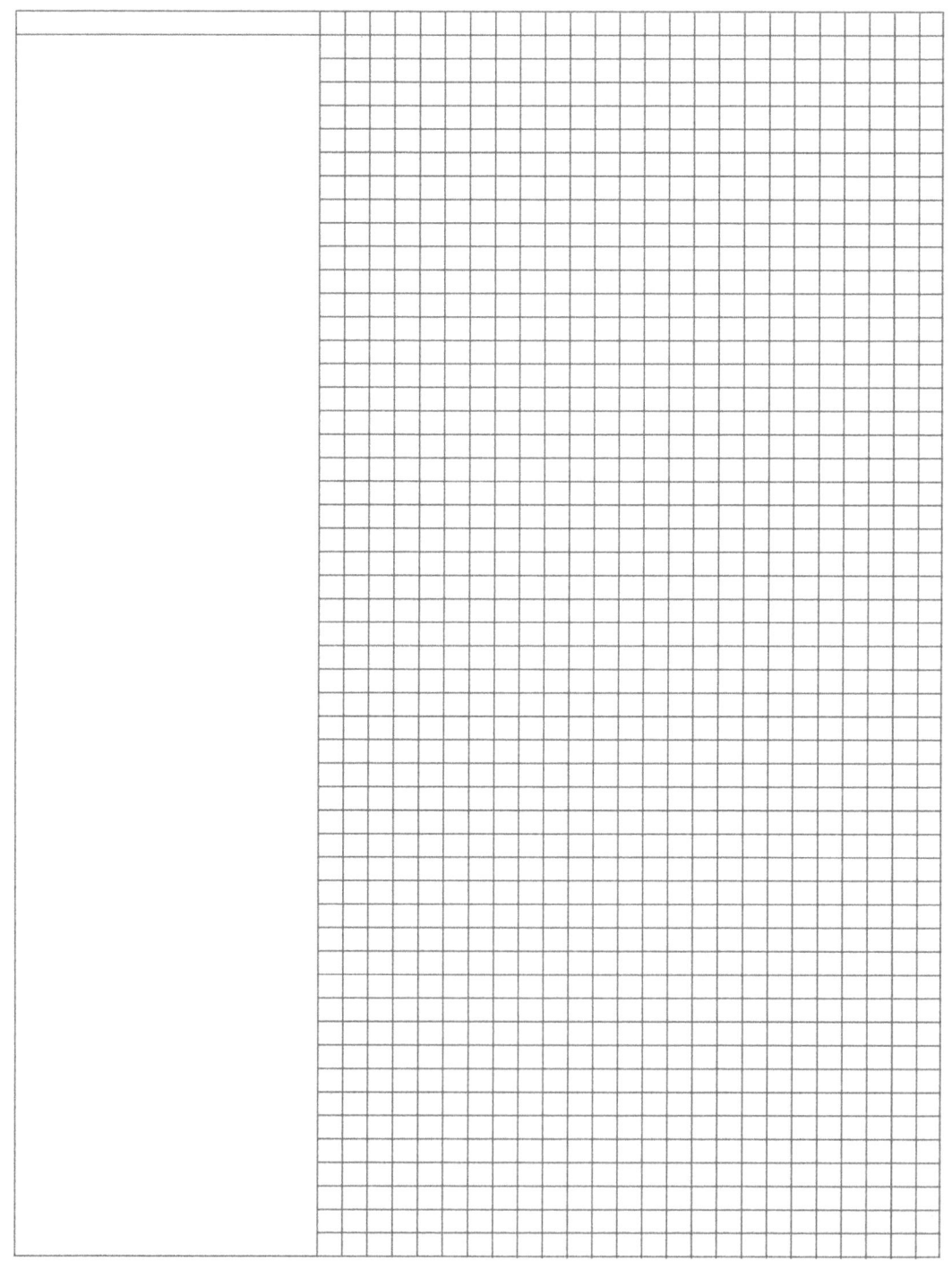

MY "BIG SHINY NEW" IDEA

My idea

....

....

....

....

....

....

Shine bright my idea. Shine bright.

SENSE CHECK:

☐ Helps with long-term plans

☐ Have the capacity to act

☐ Have the budget to act

☐ Have the skills required

What will make this idea shine?

POTENTIAL IMPACT
1 2 3 4 5 6 7 8 9 10

TIMELINE
NOW   SOON
LATER   NEVER

POTENTIAL BENEFITS   **POTENTIAL DRAWBACKS**

ACTIONED:

IMPACT:

MY "BIG SHINY NEW IDEA" PLAN

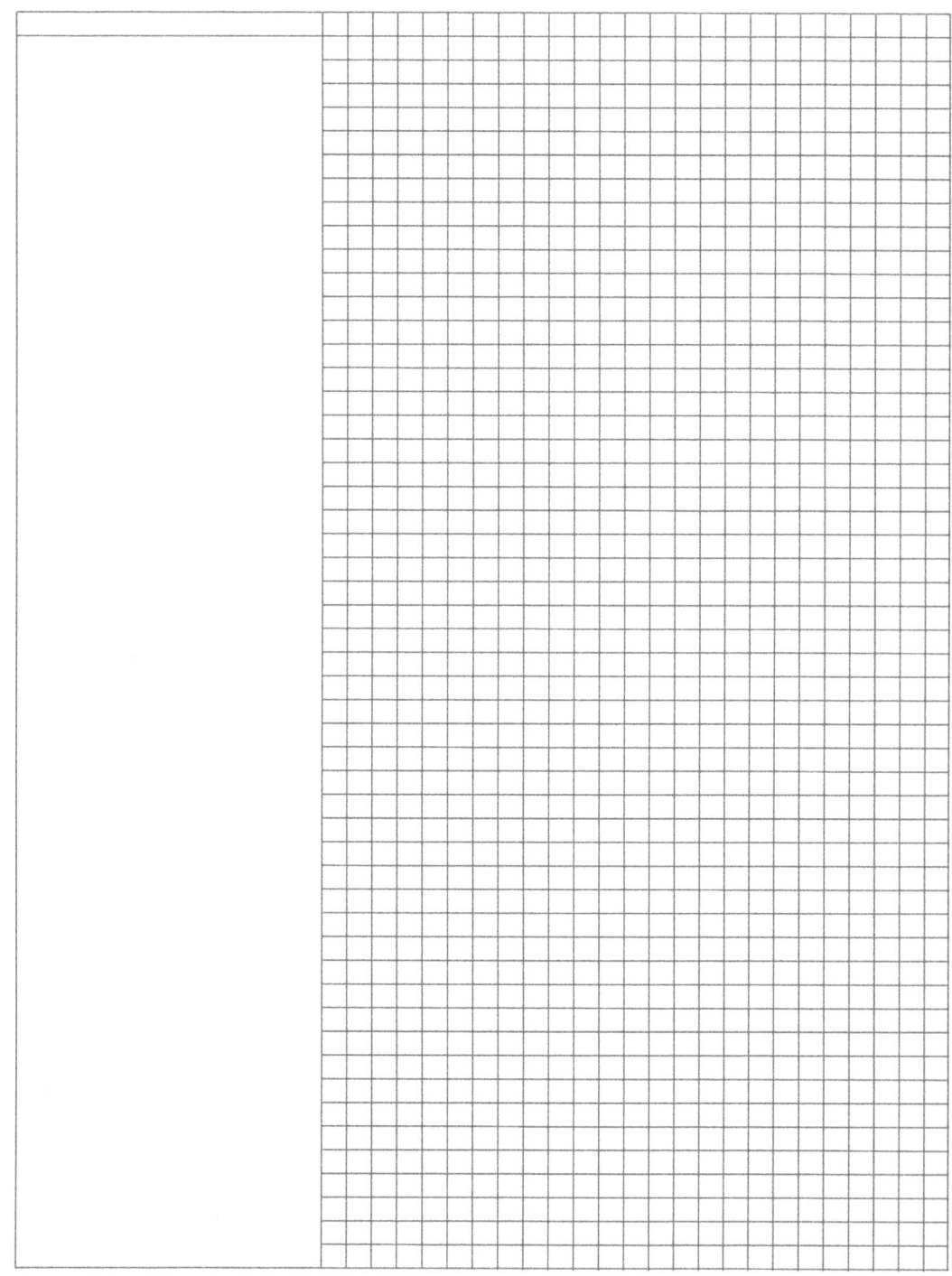

MY "BIG SHINY NEW" IDEA

My idea
....
....
....
....
....

> Shine bright my idea. Shine bright.

SENSE CHECK:

☐ Helps with long-term plans

☐ Have the capacity to act

☐ Have the budget to act

☐ Have the skills required

What will make this idea shine?

POTENTIAL IMPACT
1 2 3 4 5 6 7 8 9 10

POTENTIAL BENEFITS   **POTENTIAL DRAWBACKS**

TIMELINE
NOW   SOON
LATER NEVER

ACTIONED: **IMPACT:**

MY "BIG SHINY NEW IDEA" PLAN

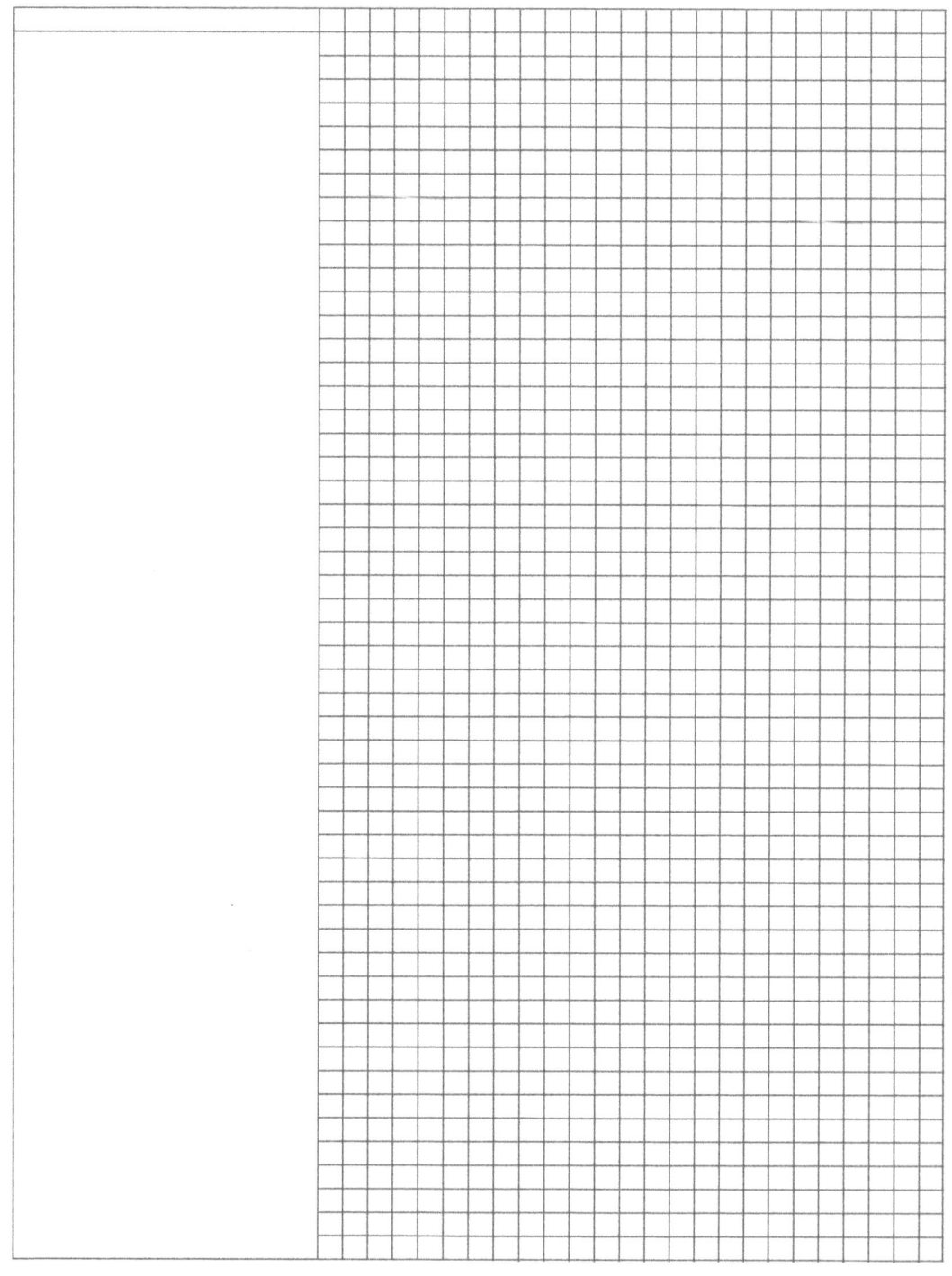

MY "BIG SHINY NEW" IDEA

My idea
....
....
....
....
....
....

> Shine bright my idea. Shine bright.

SENSE CHECK:

- ☐ Helps with long-term plans
- ☐ Have the capacity to act
- ☐ Have the budget to act
- ☐ Have the skills required

What will make this idea shine?

POTENTIAL IMPACT
1 2 3 4 5 6 7 8 9 10

TIMELINE
NOW   SOON
LATER NEVER

POTENTIAL BENEFITS	POTENTIAL DRAWBACKS

ACTIONED:

IMPACT:

MY "BIG SHINY NEW IDEA" PLAN

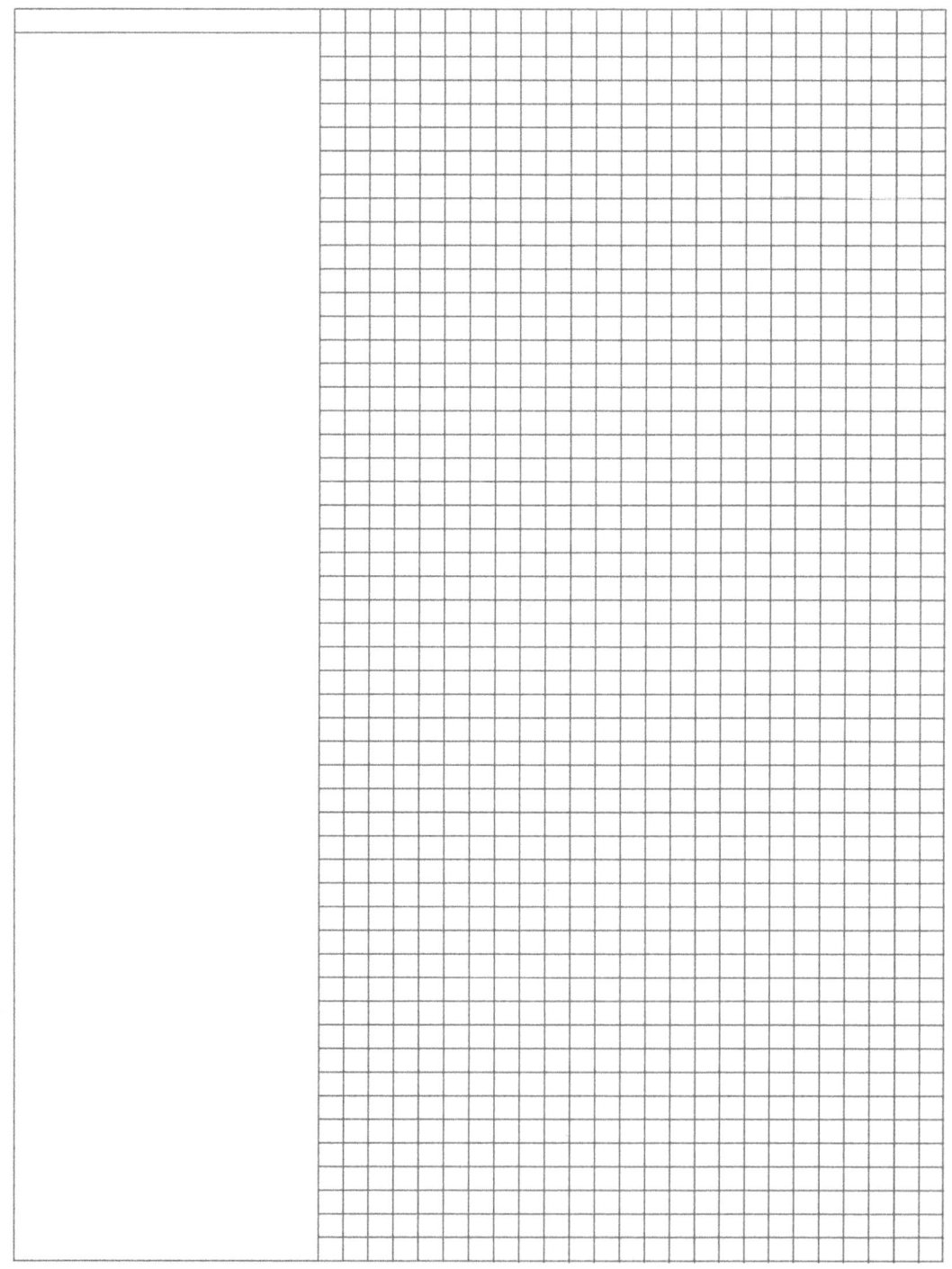

MY "BIG SHINY NEW" IDEA

My idea
....
....
....
....
....
....

Shine bright my idea. Shine bright.

SENSE CHECK:

☐ Helps with long-term plans

☐ Have the capacity to act

☐ Have the budget to act

☐ Have the skills required

POTENTIAL IMPACT
1 2 3 4 5 6 7 8 9 10

TIMELINE
NOW   SOON
LATER NEVER

What will make this idea shine?

POTENTIAL BENEFITS   POTENTIAL DRAWBACKS

ACTIONED:

IMPACT:

MY "BIG SHINY NEW IDEA" PLAN

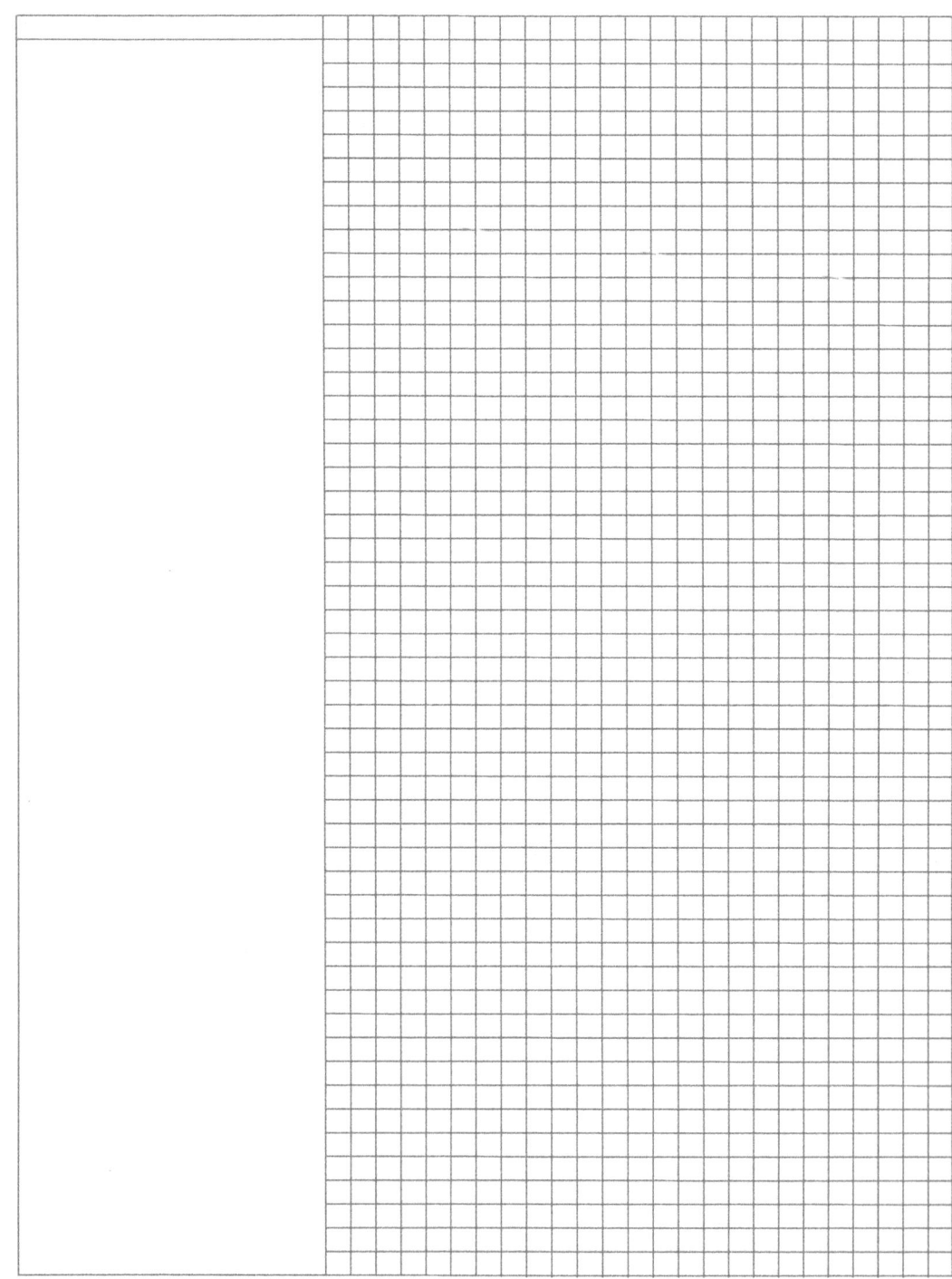

MY "BIG SHINY NEW" IDEA

My idea

....

....

....

....

....

....

> Shine bright my idea. Shine bright.

SENSE CHECK:

☐ Helps with long-term plans

☐ Have the capacity to act

☐ Have the budget to act

☐ Have the skills required

What will make this idea shine?

POTENTIAL IMPACT
1 2 3 4 5 6 7 8 9 10

TIMELINE
NOW   SOON
LATER   NEVER

POTENTIAL BENEFITS   POTENTIAL DRAWBACKS

ACTIONED:

IMPACT:

MY "BIG SHINY NEW IDEA" PLAN

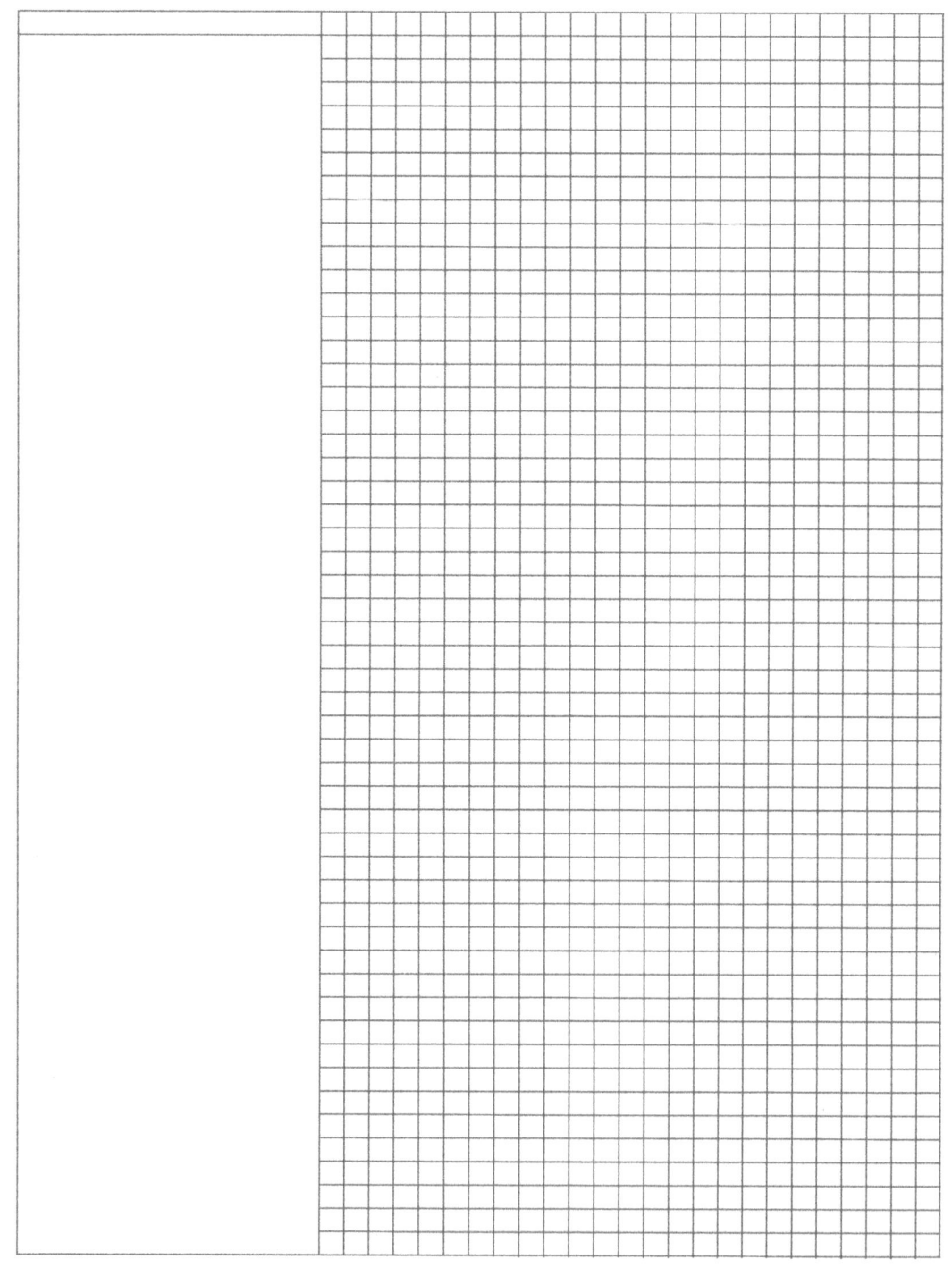

MY "BIG SHINY NEW" IDEA

My idea

....

....

....

....

....

....

> Shine bright my idea. Shine bright.

SENSE CHECK:

☐ Helps with long-term plans

☐ Have the capacity to act

☐ Have the budget to act

☐ Have the skills required

What will make this idea shine?

POTENTIAL IMPACT
1 2 3 4 5 6 7 8 9 10

TIMELINE
NOW   SOON
LATER   NEVER

POTENTIAL BENEFITS   POTENTIAL DRAWBACKS

ACTIONED:

IMPACT:

MY "BIG SHINY NEW IDEA" PLAN

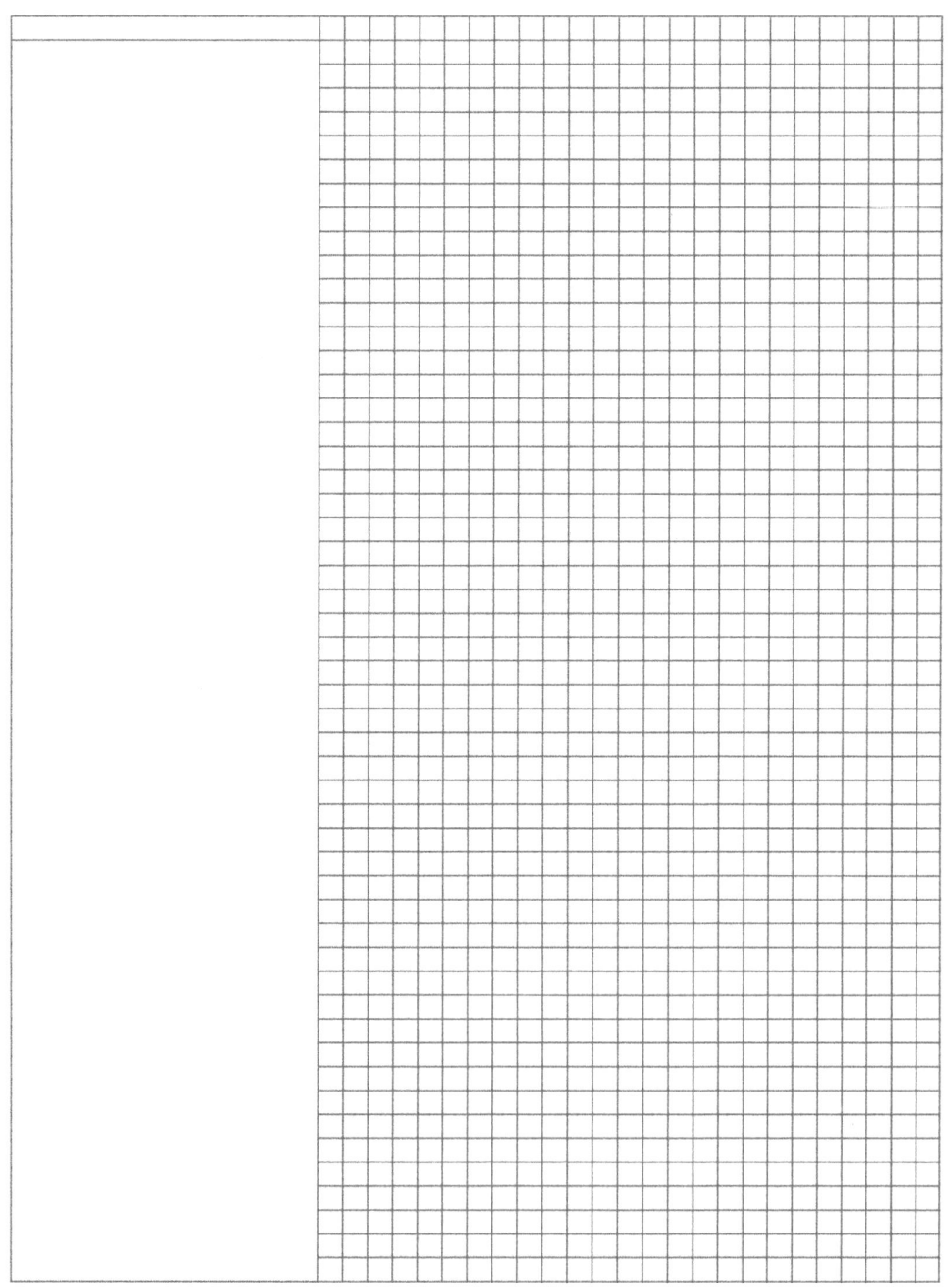

MY "BIG SHINY NEW" IDEA

My idea
....
....
....
....
....

Shine bright my idea. Shine bright.

SENSE CHECK:

☐ Helps with long-term plans
☐ Have the capacity to act
☐ Have the budget to act
☐ Have the skills required

What will make this idea shine?

POTENTIAL IMPACT
1 2 3 4 5 6 7 8 9 10

TIMELINE
NOW   SOON
LATER   NEVER

POTENTIAL BENEFITS   POTENTIAL DRAWBACKS

ACTIONED:

IMPACT:

MY "BIG SHINY NEW IDEA" PLAN

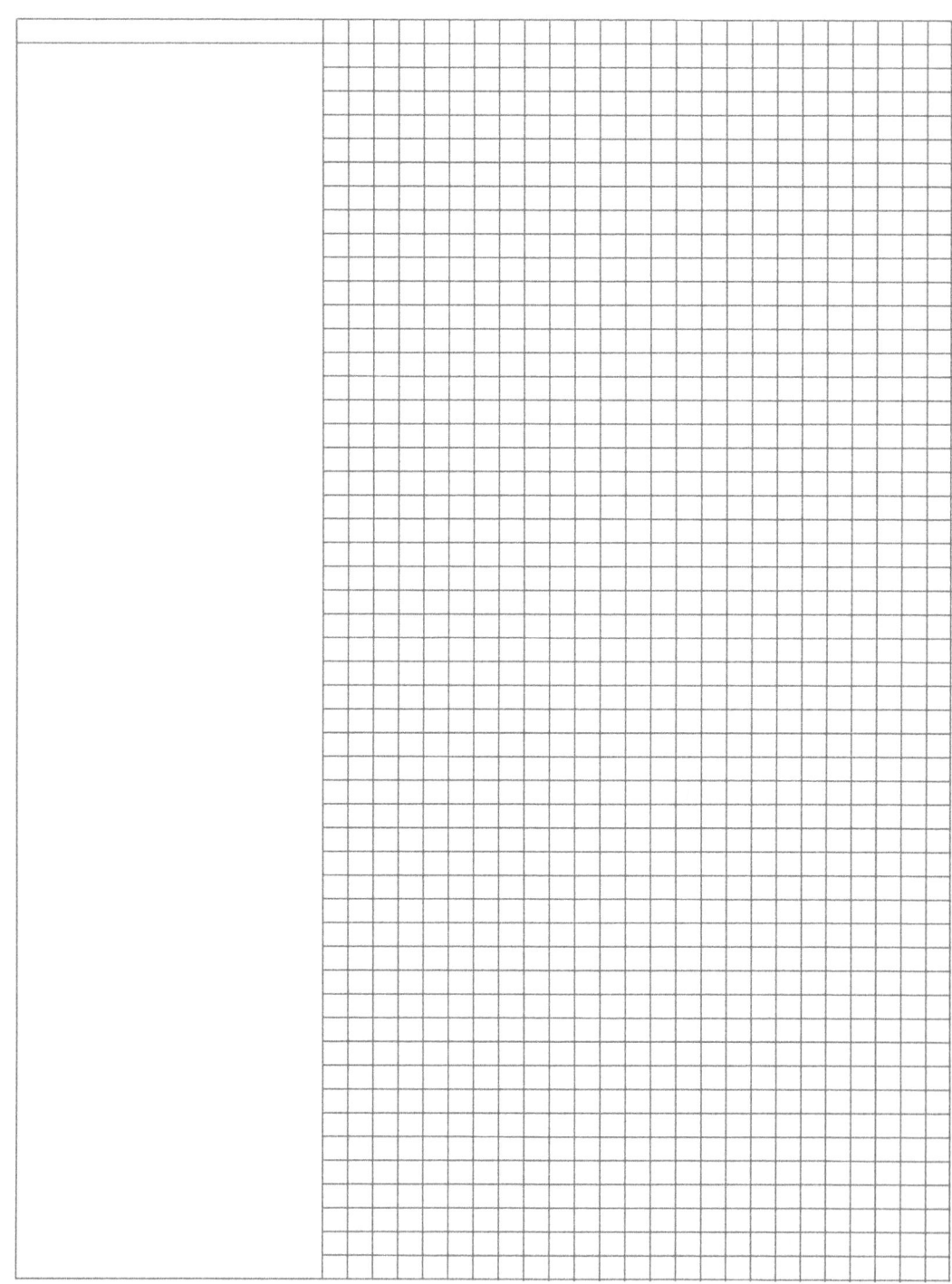

MY "BIG SHINY NEW" IDEA

My idea
....
....
....
....
....
....

Shine bright my idea. Shine bright.

SENSE CHECK:

☐ Helps with long-term plans

☐ Have the capacity to act

☐ Have the budget to act

☐ Have the skills required

What will make this idea shine?

POTENTIAL IMPACT
1 2 3 4 5 6 7 8 9 10

TIMELINE
NOW   SOON
LATER NEVER

POTENTIAL BENEFITS   **POTENTIAL DRAWBACKS**

ACTIONED: **IMPACT:**

MY "BIG SHINY NEW IDEA" PLAN

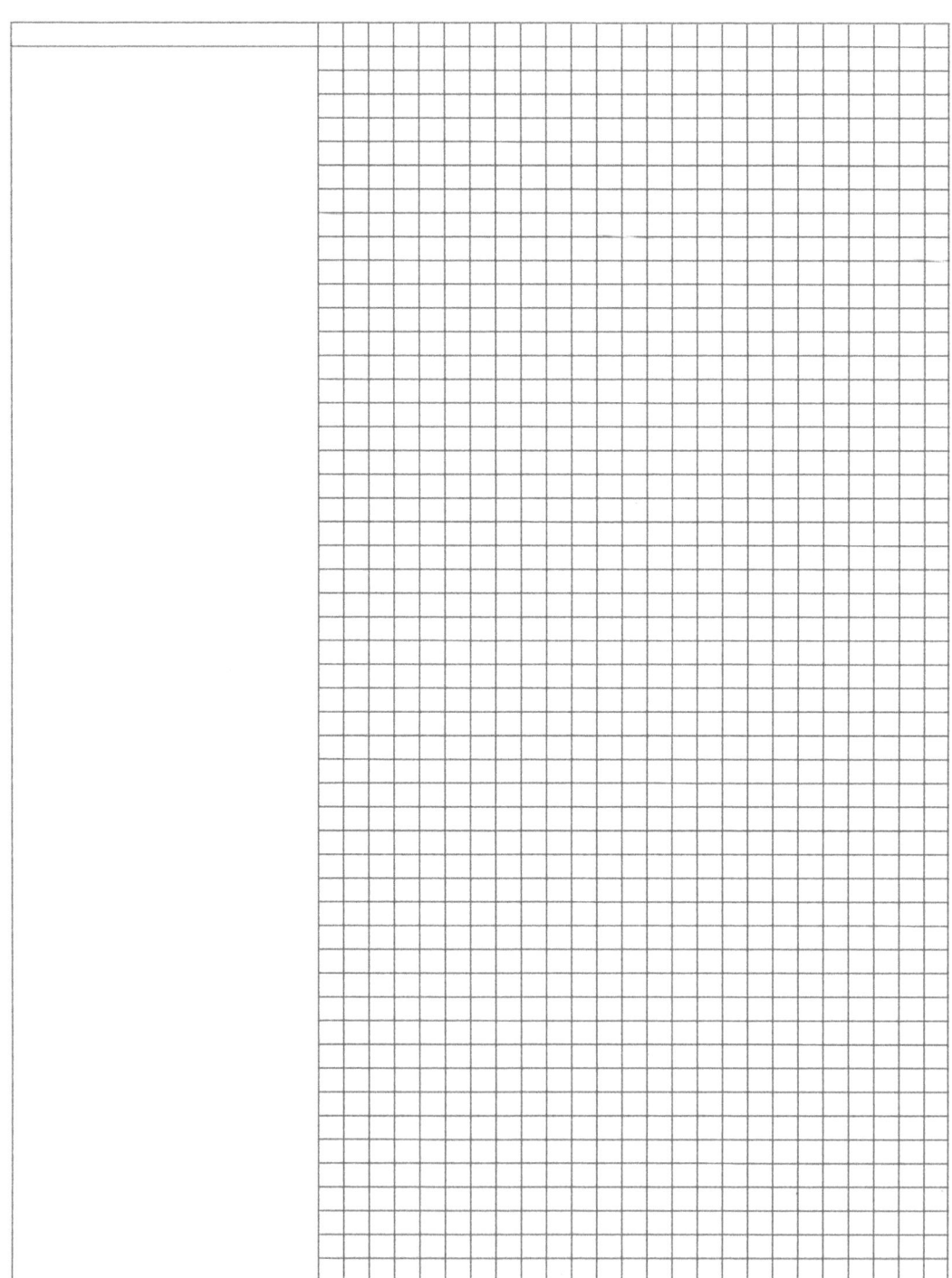

MY "BIG SHINY NEW" IDEA

My idea

....

....

....

....

....

....

> Shine bright my idea. Shine bright.

SENSE CHECK:

☐ Helps with long-term plans

☐ Have the capacity to act

☐ Have the budget to act

☐ Have the skills required

POTENTIAL IMPACT
1 2 3 4 5 6 7 8 9 10

TIMELINE
NOW   SOON
LATER NEVER

What will make this idea shine?

POTENTIAL BENEFITS   POTENTIAL DRAWBACKS

ACTIONED:

IMPACT:

MY "BIG SHINY NEW IDEA" PLAN

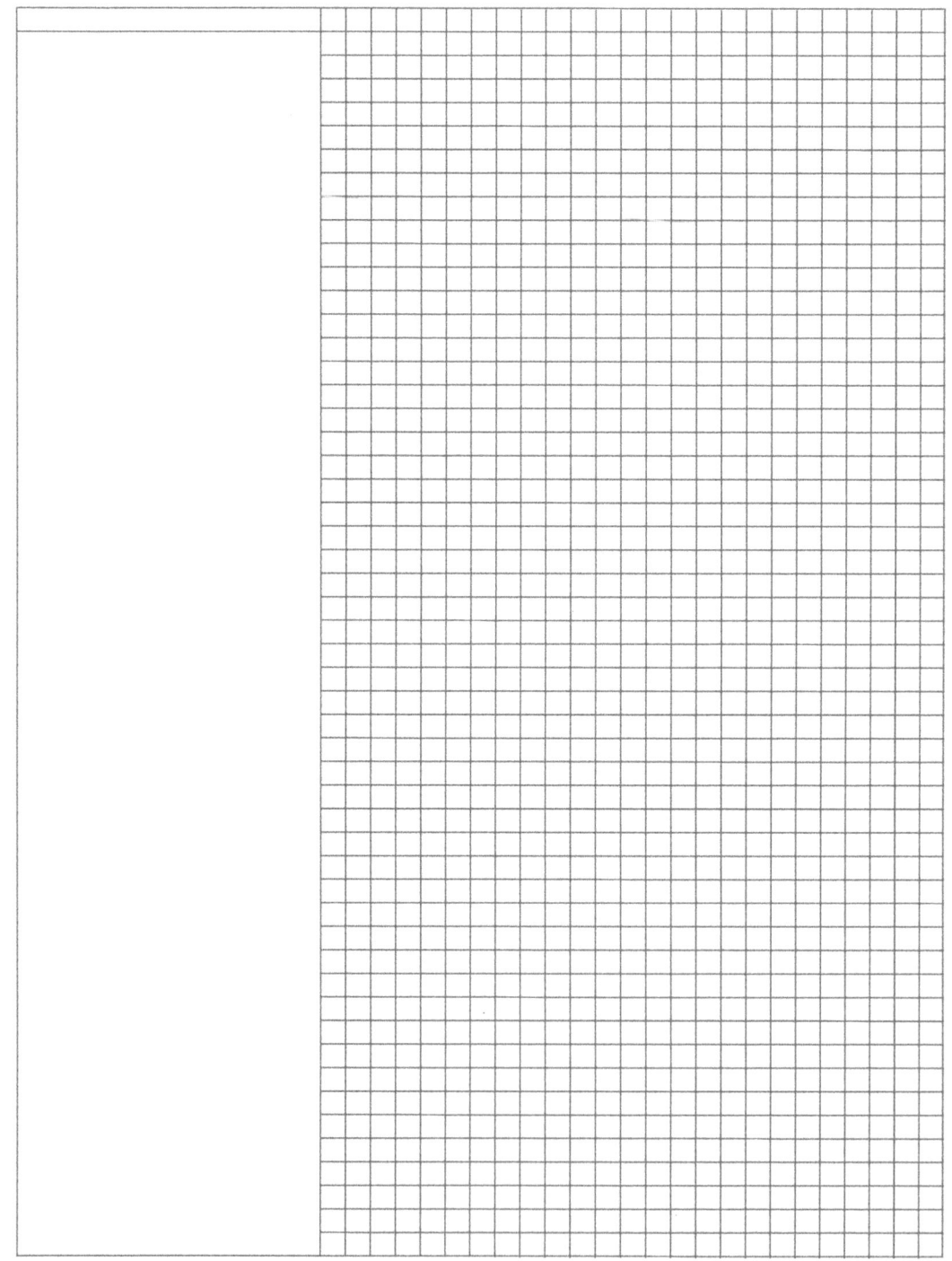

MY "BIG SHINY NEW" IDEA

My idea

....

....

....

....

....

....

Shine bright my idea. Shine bright.

SENSE CHECK:

☐ Helps with long-term plans

☐ Have the capacity to act

☐ Have the budget to act

☐ Have the skills required

What will make this idea shine?

POTENTIAL IMPACT
1 2 3 4 5 6 7 8 9 10

TIMELINE
NOW   SOON
LATER NEVER

POTENTIAL BENEFITS   POTENTIAL DRAWBACKS

ACTIONED:

IMPACT:

MY "BIG SHINY NEW IDEA" PLAN

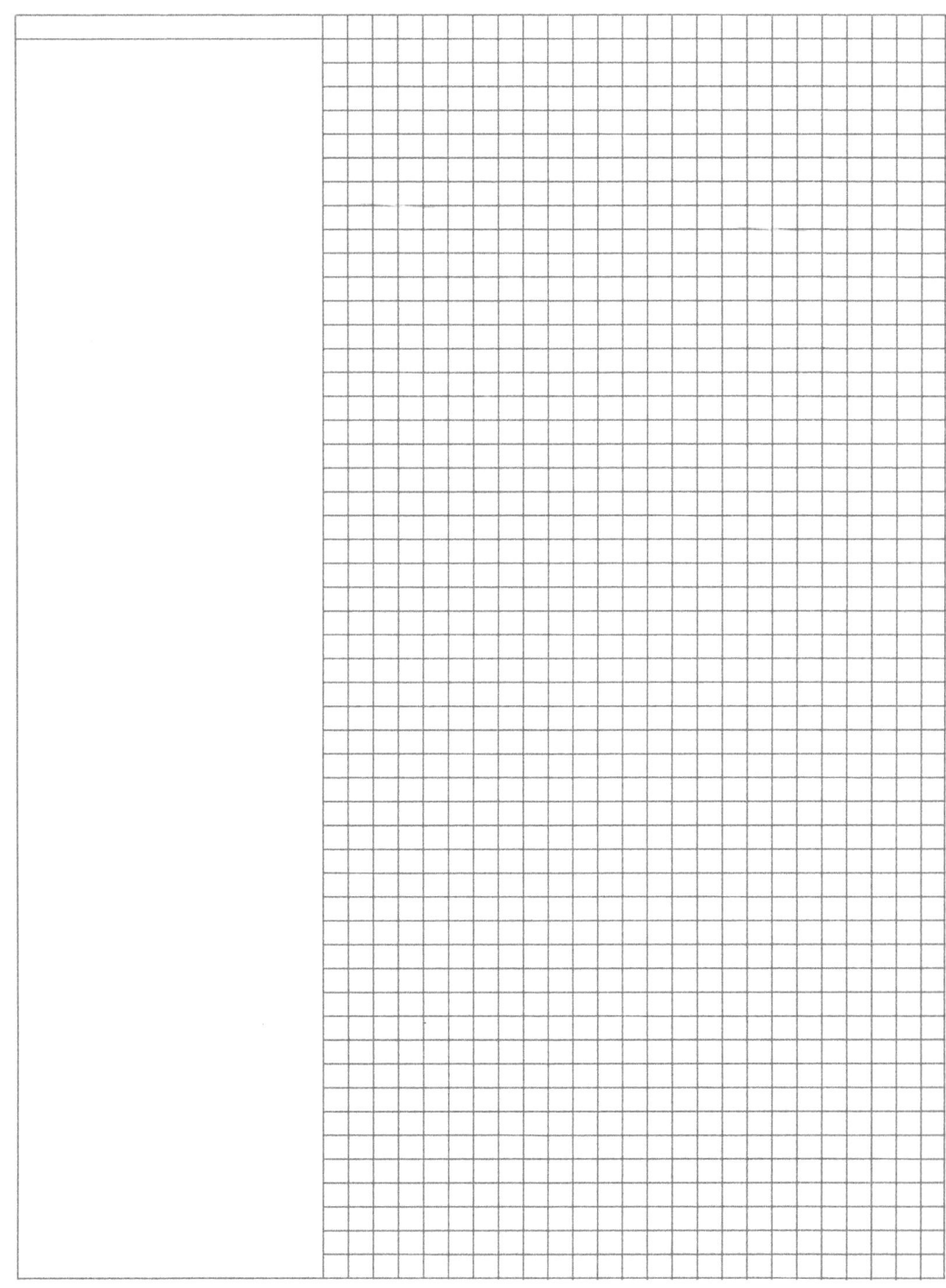

MY "BIG SHINY NEW" IDEA

My idea

....

....

....

....

....

Shine bright my idea. Shine bright.

SENSE CHECK:

☐ Helps with long-term plans

☐ Have the capacity to act

☐ Have the budget to act

☐ Have the skills required

What will make this idea shine?

POTENTIAL IMPACT
1 2 3 4 5 6 7 8 9 10

TIMELINE
NOW   SOON
LATER   NEVER

POTENTIAL BENEFITS   POTENTIAL DRAWBACKS

ACTIONED:

IMPACT:

MY "BIG SHINY NEW IDEA" PLAN

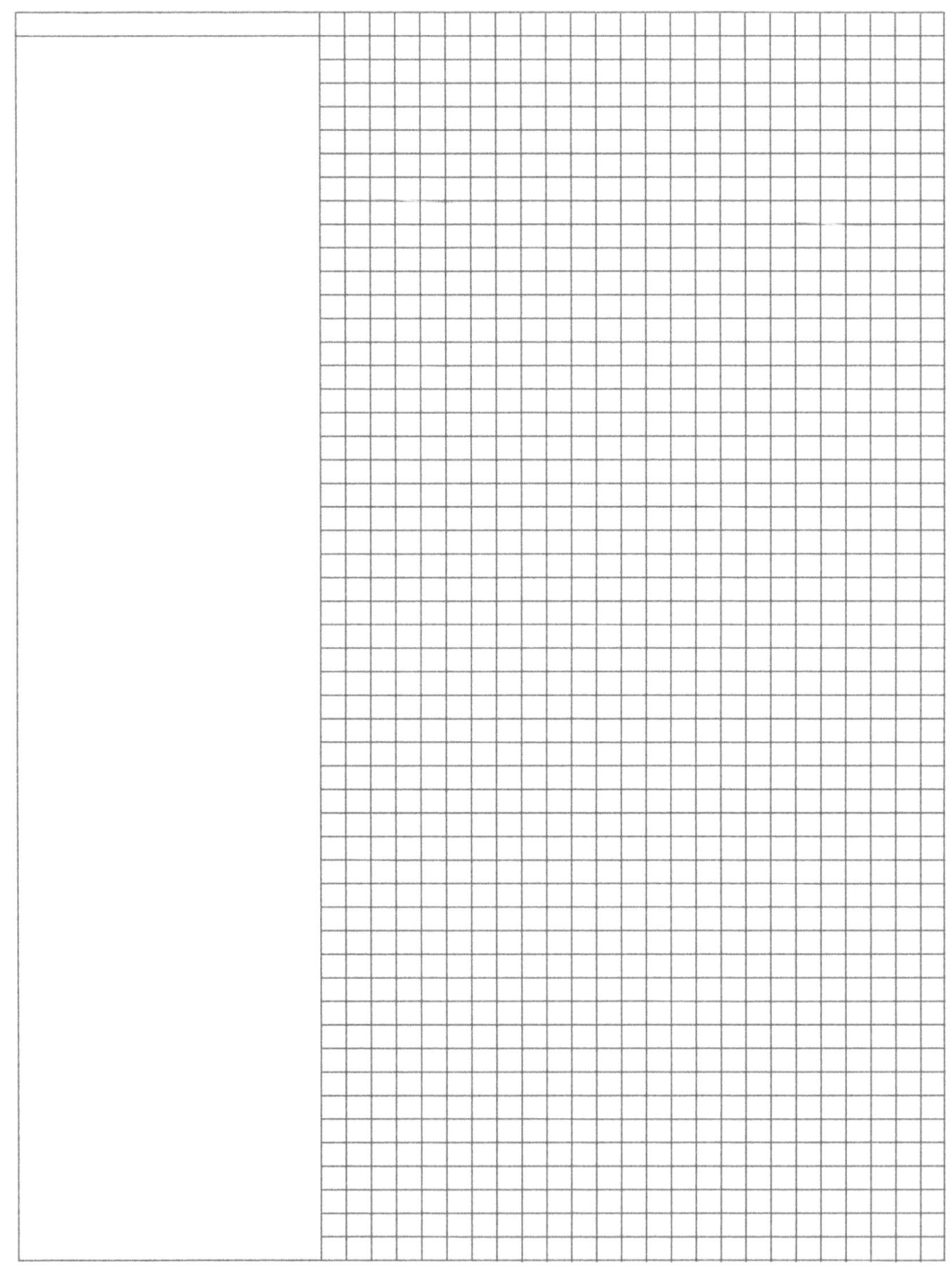

MY "BIG SHINY NEW" IDEA

My idea

....

....

....

....

....

....

Shine bright my idea. Shine bright.

SENSE CHECK:

☐ Helps with long-term plans

☐ Have the capacity to act

☐ Have the budget to act

☐ Have the skills required

What will make this idea shine?

POTENTIAL IMPACT
1 2 3 4 5 6 7 8 9 10

TIMELINE
NOW   SOON
LATER   NEVER

POTENTIAL BENEFITS   POTENTIAL DRAWBACKS

ACTIONED:

IMPACT:

MY "BIG SHINY NEW IDEA" PLAN

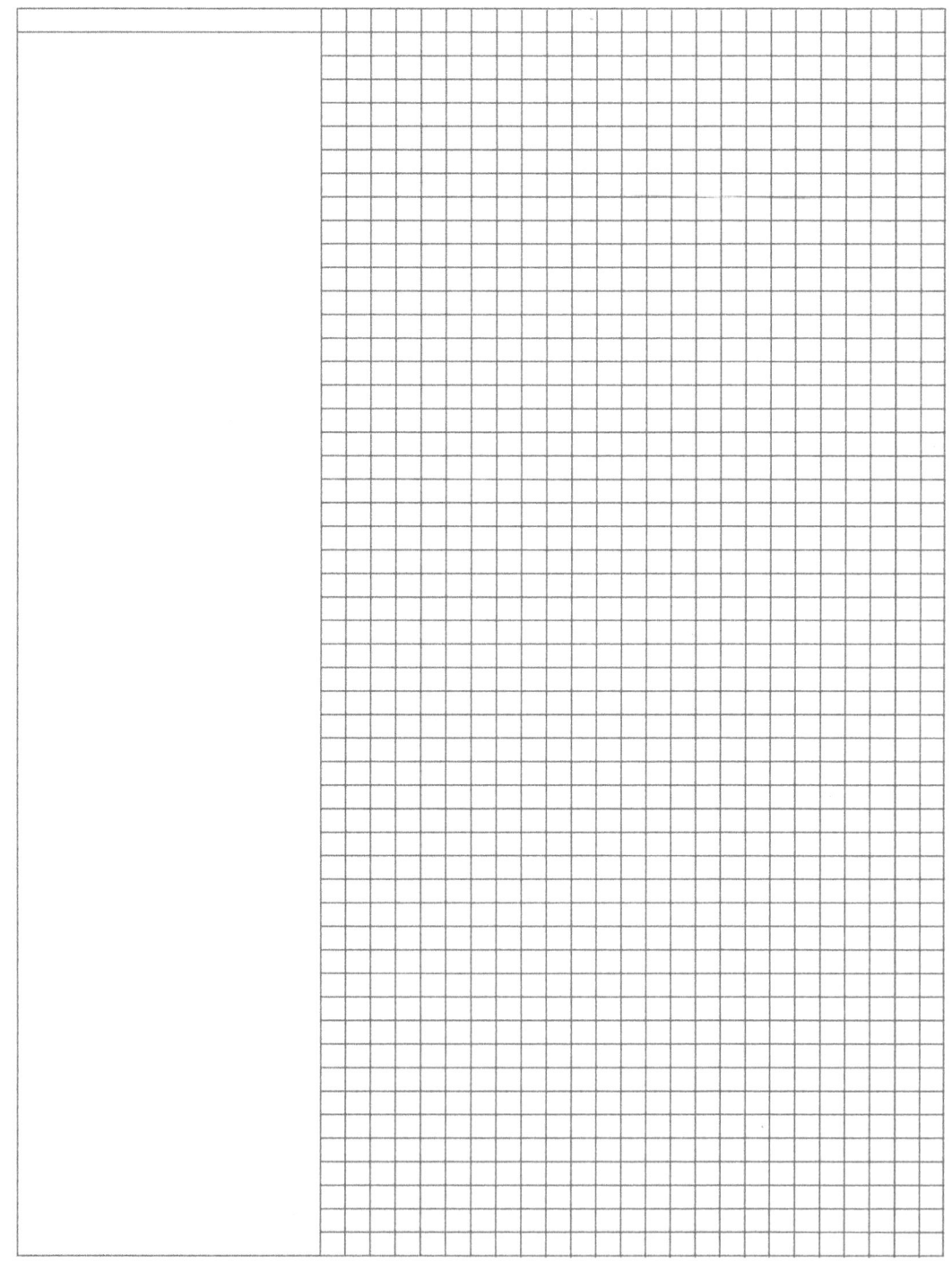

MY "BIG SHINY NEW" IDEA

My idea
....
....
....
....
....

Shine bright my idea. Shine bright.

SENSE CHECK:

☐ Helps with long-term plans
☐ Have the capacity to act
☐ Have the budget to act
☐ Have the skills required

What will make this idea shine?

POTENTIAL IMPACT
1 2 3 4 5 6 7 8 9 10

TIMELINE
NOW   SOON
LATER   NEVER

POTENTIAL BENEFITS   POTENTIAL DRAWBACKS

ACTIONED:

IMPACT:

MY "BIG SHINY NEW IDEA" PLAN

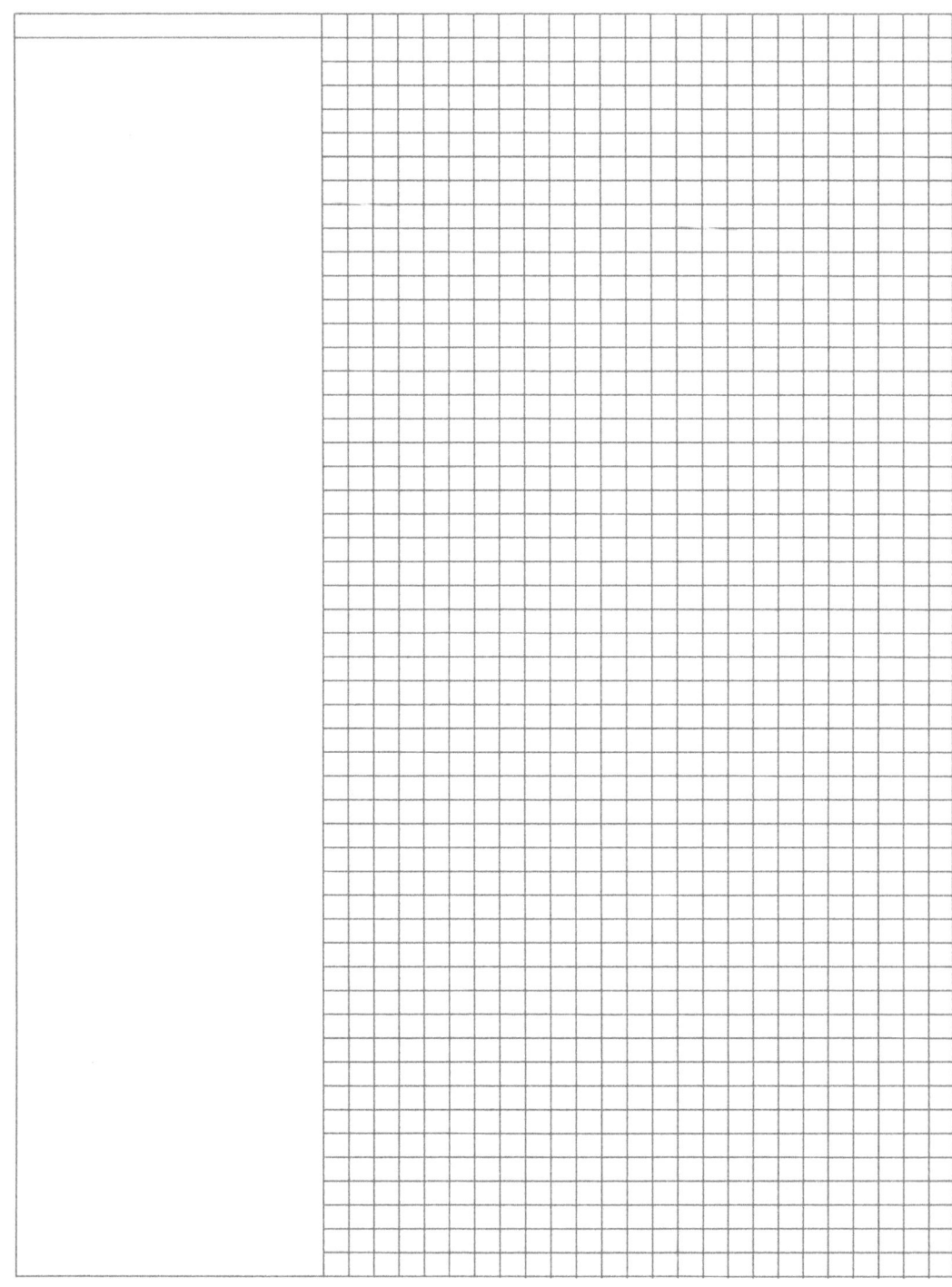

MY "BIG SHINY NEW" IDEA

My idea
....
....
....
....
....

Shine bright my idea. Shine bright.

SENSE CHECK:

☐ Helps with long-term plans
☐ Have the capacity to act
☐ Have the budget to act
☐ Have the skills required

What will make this idea shine?

POTENTIAL IMPACT
1 2 3 4 5 6 7 8 9 10

TIMELINE
NOW   SOON
LATER   NEVER

POTENTIAL BENEFITS   POTENTIAL DRAWBACKS

ACTIONED:

IMPACT:

MY "BIG SHINY NEW IDEA" PLAN

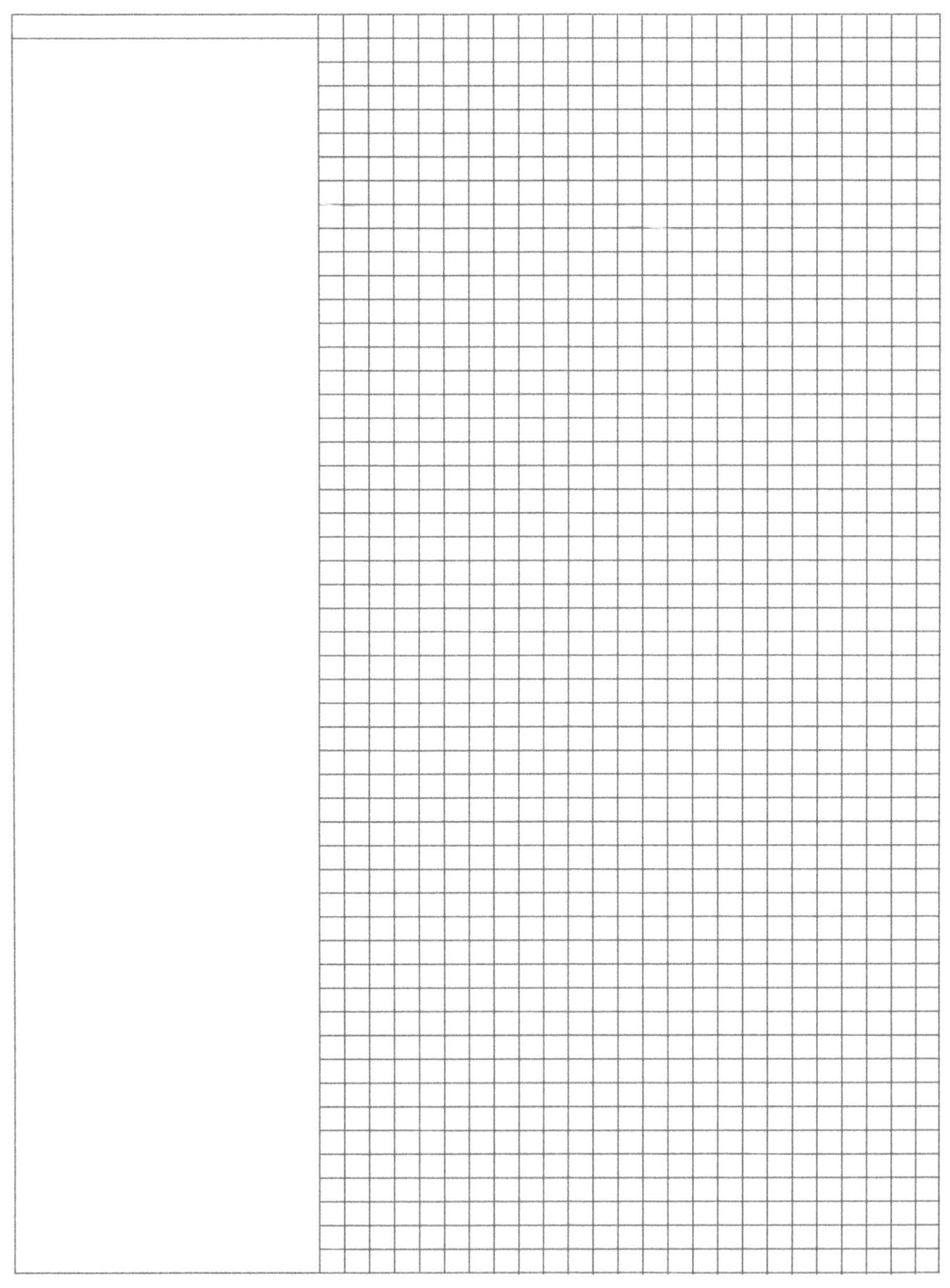

MY "BIG SHINY NEW" IDEA

My idea
....
....
....
....
....
....

> Shine bright my idea. Shine bright.

SENSE CHECK:

- ☐ Helps with long-term plans
- ☐ Have the capacity to act
- ☐ Have the budget to act
- ☐ Have the skills required

What will make this idea shine?

POTENTIAL IMPACT
1 2 3 4 5 6 7 8 9 10

POTENTIAL BENEFITS   **POTENTIAL DRAWBACKS**

TIMELINE
NOW   SOON
LATER NEVER

ACTIONED:

IMPACT:

MY "BIG SHINY NEW IDEA" PLAN

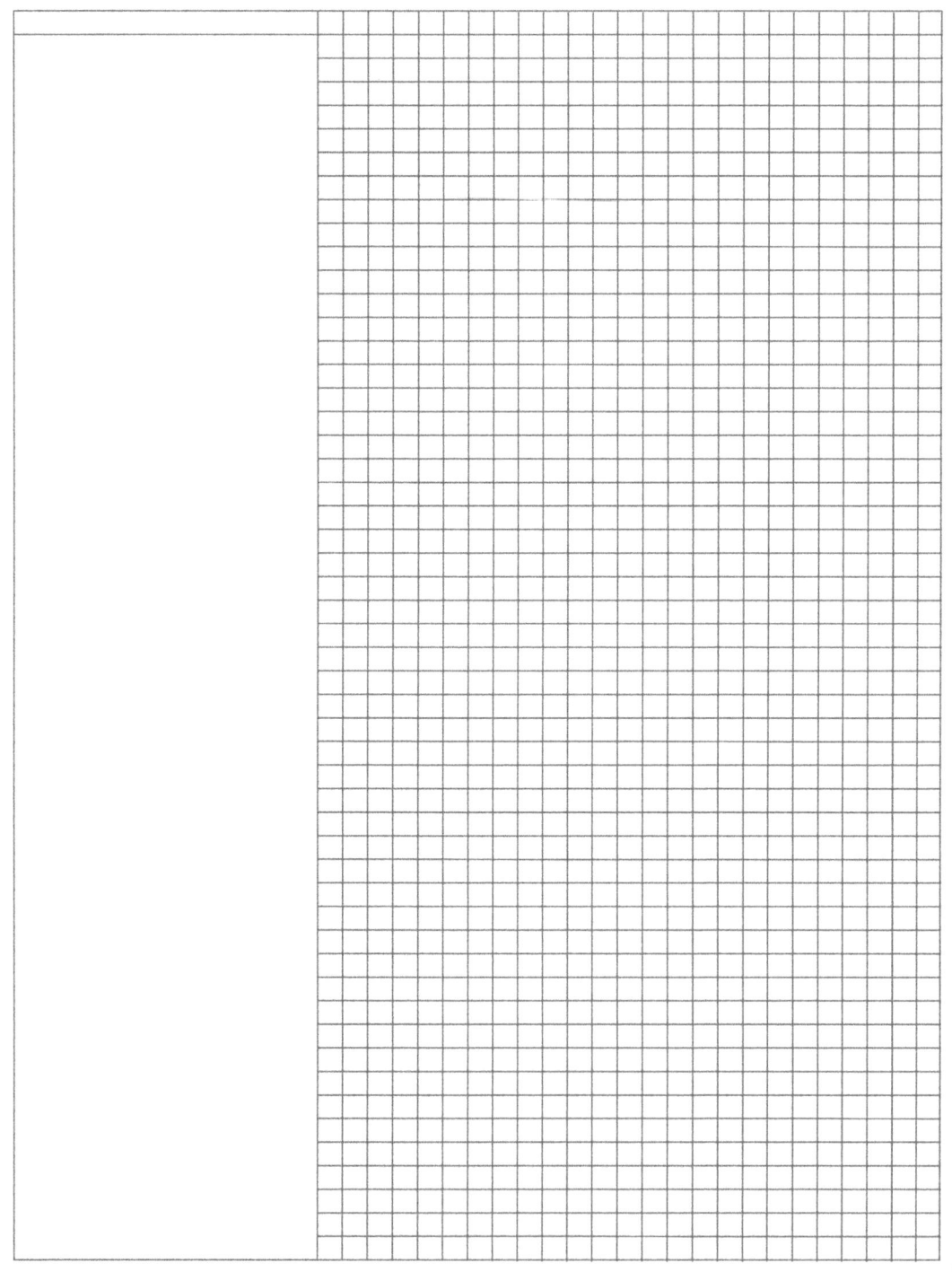

MY "BIG SHINY NEW" IDEA

My idea

....

....

....

....

....

....

Shine bright my idea. Shine bright.

SENSE CHECK:

☐ Helps with long-term plans

☐ Have the capacity to act

☐ Have the budget to act

☐ Have the skills required

POTENTIAL IMPACT
1 2 3 4 5 6 7 8 9 10

TIMELINE
NOW   SOON
LATER   NEVER

What will make this idea shine?

POTENTIAL BENEFITS   POTENTIAL DRAWBACKS

ACTIONED: **IMPACT:**

MY "BIG SHINY NEW IDEA" PLAN

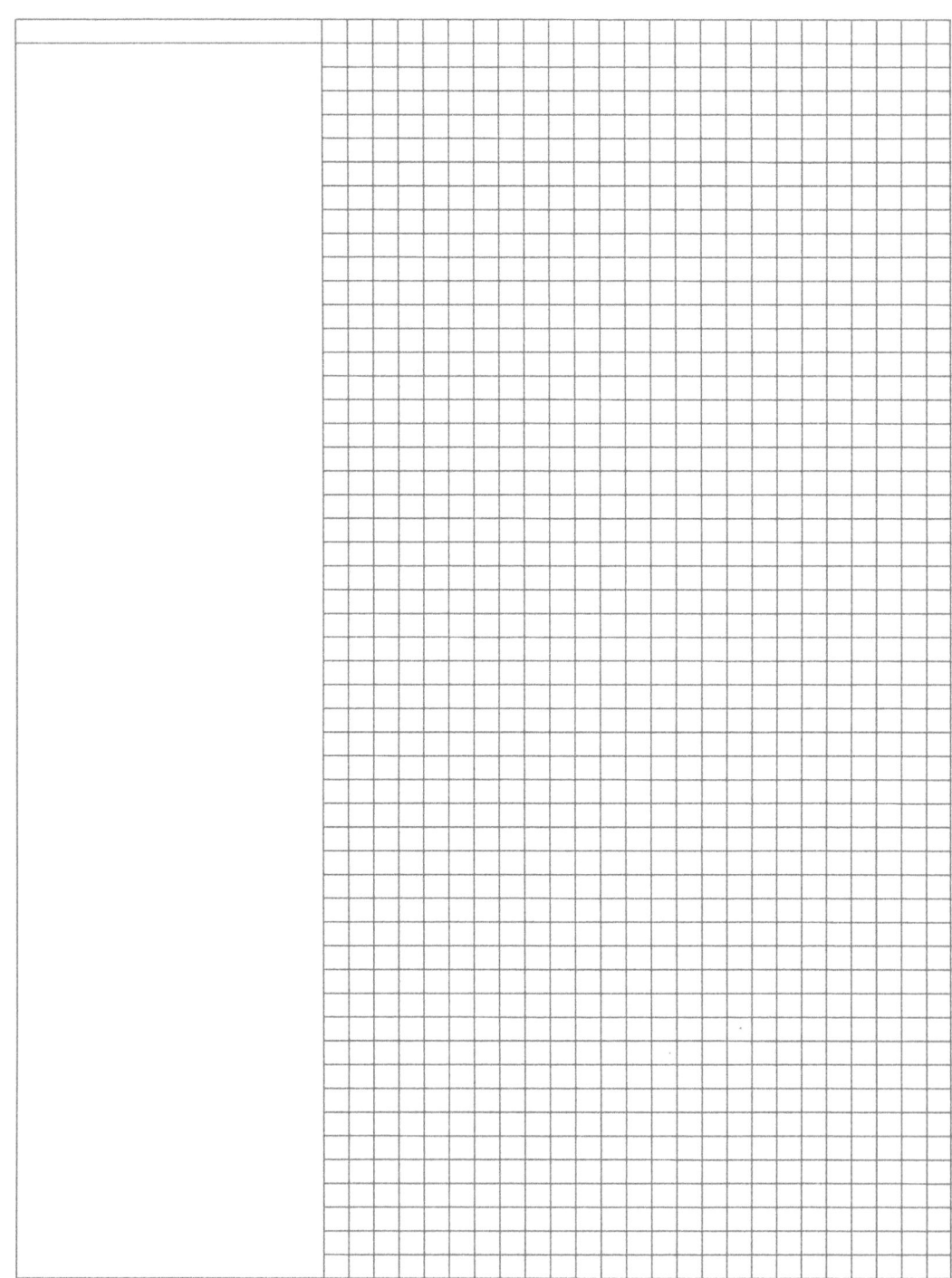

MY "BIG SHINY NEW" IDEA

My idea
....
....
....
....
....
....

Shine bright my idea. Shine bright.

SENSE CHECK:

- ☐ Helps with long-term plans
- ☐ Have the capacity to act
- ☐ Have the budget to act
- ☐ Have the skills required

What will make this idea shine?

POTENTIAL IMPACT
1 2 3 4 5 6 7 8 9 10

TIMELINE
NOW   SOON
LATER NEVER

POTENTIAL BENEFITS   **POTENTIAL DRAWBACKS**

ACTIONED: **IMPACT:**

MY "BIG SHINY NEW IDEA" PLAN

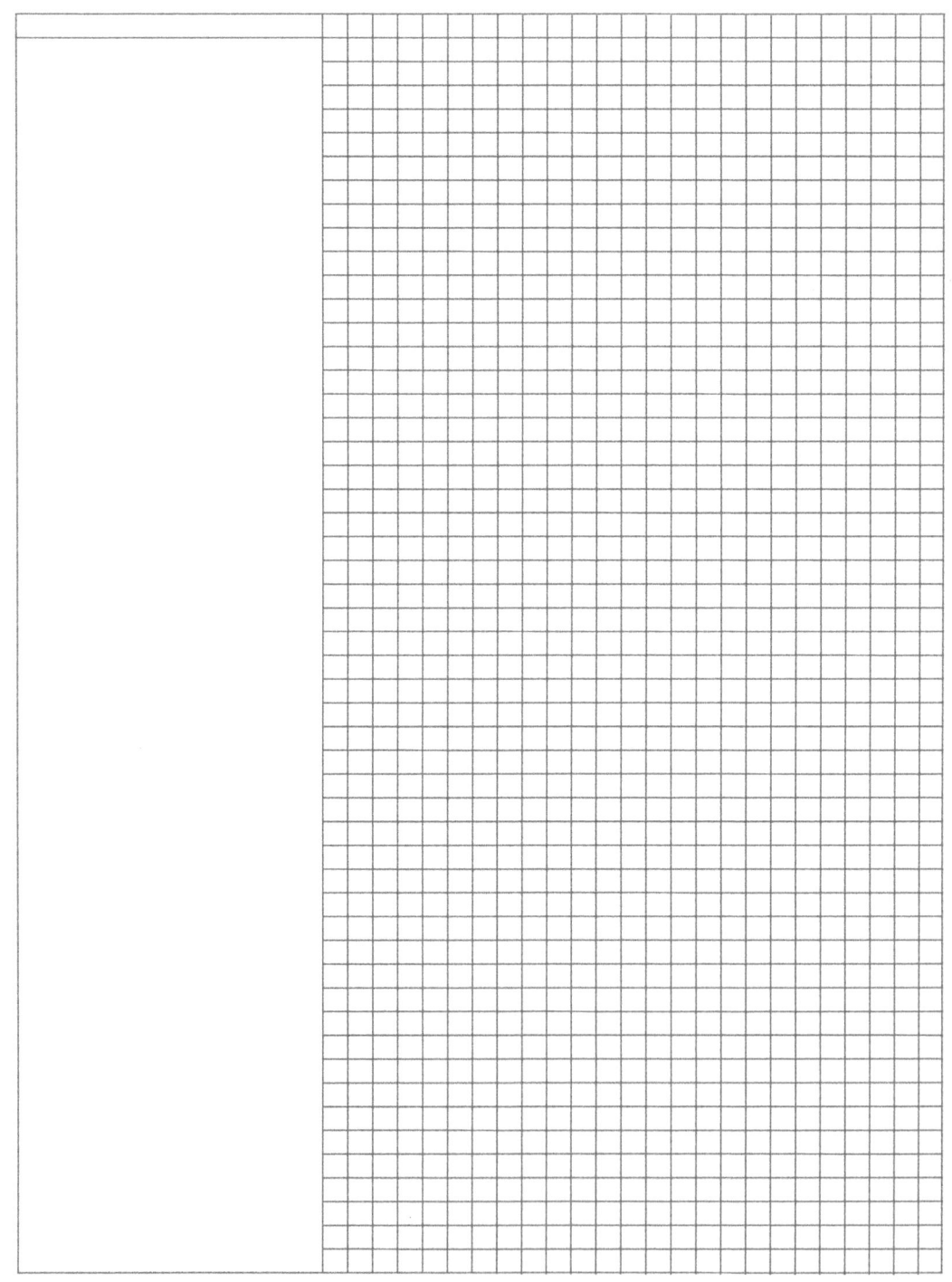

MY "BIG SHINY NEW" IDEA

My idea
....
....
....
....
....
....

Shine bright my idea. Shine bright.

SENSE CHECK:

☐ Helps with long-term plans
☐ Have the capacity to act
☐ Have the budget to act
☐ Have the skills required

What will make this idea shine?

POTENTIAL IMPACT
1 2 3 4 5 6 7 8 9 10

TIMELINE
NOW   SOON
LATER   NEVER

POTENTIAL BENEFITS   POTENTIAL DRAWBACKS

ACTIONED:

IMPACT:

MY "BIG SHINY NEW IDEA" PLAN

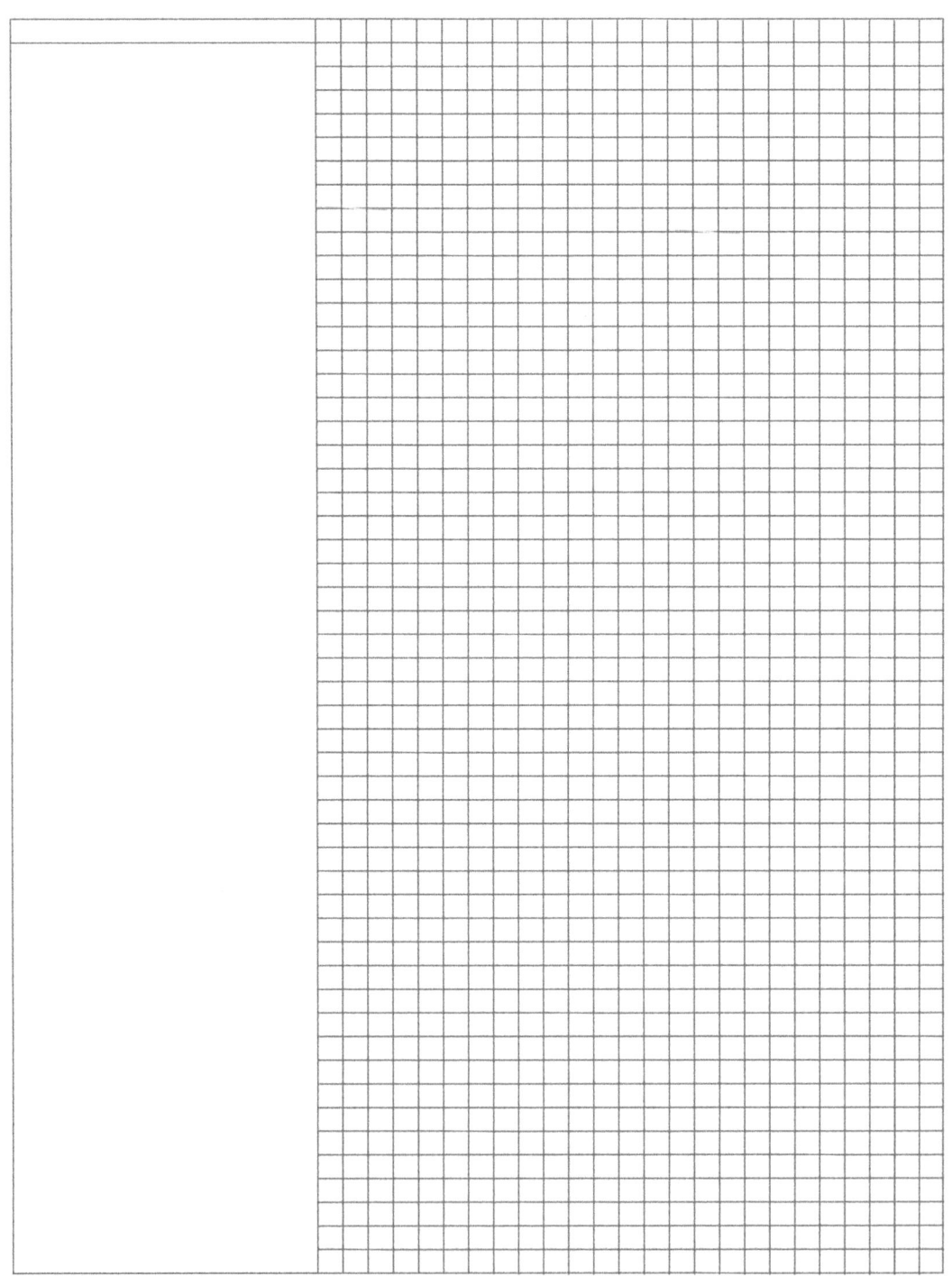

MY "BIG SHINY NEW" IDEA

My idea
....
....
....
....
....

Shine bright my idea. Shine bright.

SENSE CHECK:

☐ Helps with long-term plans
☐ Have the capacity to act
☐ Have the budget to act
☐ Have the skills required

What will make this idea shine?

POTENTIAL IMPACT
1 2 3 4 5 6 7 8 9 10

TIMELINE
NOW   SOON
LATER NEVER

POTENTIAL BENEFITS   **POTENTIAL DRAWBACKS**

ACTIONED:

IMPACT:

MY "BIG SHINY NEW IDEA" PLAN

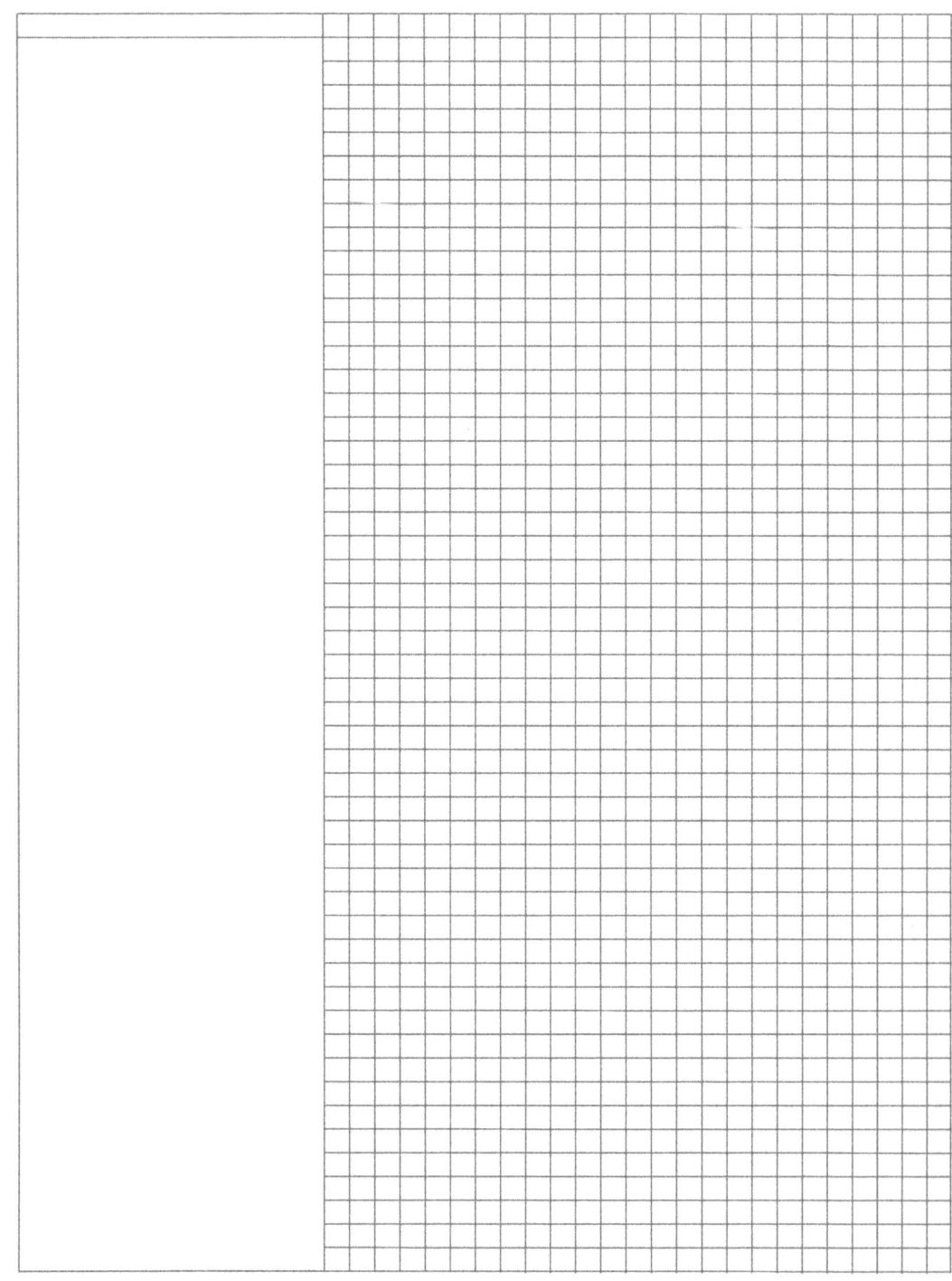

MY "BIG SHINY NEW" IDEA

My idea

....

....

....

....

....

....

Shine bright my idea. Shine bright.

SENSE CHECK:

☐ Helps with long-term plans

☐ Have the capacity to act

☐ Have the budget to act

☐ Have the skills required

What will make this idea shine?

POTENTIAL IMPACT
1 2 3 4 5 6 7 8 9 10

TIMELINE
NOW   SOON
LATER   NEVER

POTENTIAL BENEFITS   POTENTIAL DRAWBACKS

ACTIONED:

IMPACT:

MY "BIG SHINY NEW IDEA" PLAN

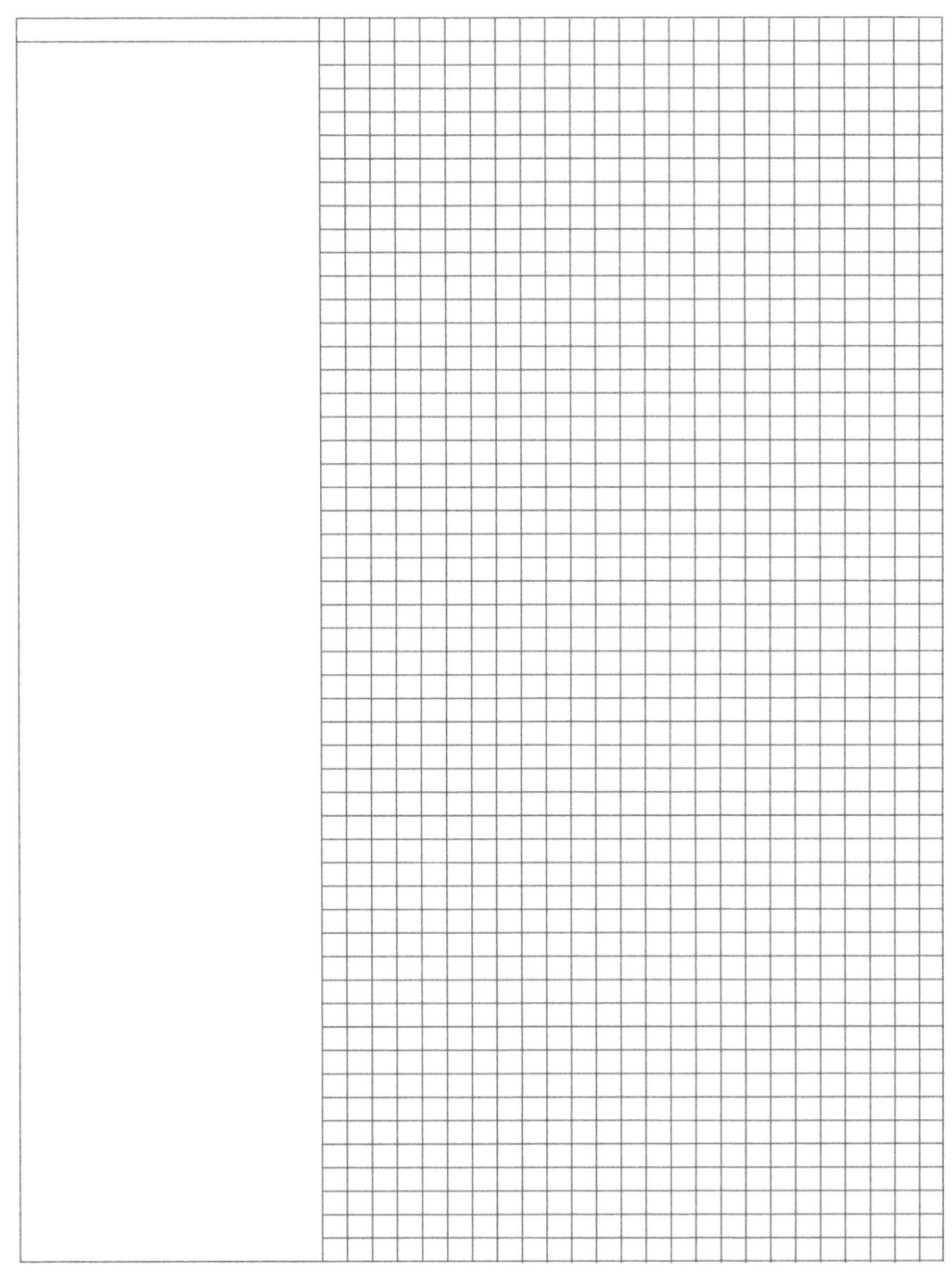

MY "BIG SHINY NEW" IDEA

My idea

....

....

....

....

....

....

> Shine bright my idea. Shine bright.

SENSE CHECK:

☐ Helps with long-term plans

☐ Have the capacity to act

☐ Have the budget to act

☐ Have the skills required

What will make this idea shine?

POTENTIAL IMPACT
1 2 3 4 5 6 7 8 9 10

POTENTIAL BENEFITS   **POTENTIAL DRAWBACKS**

TIMELINE
NOW   SOON
LATER   NEVER

ACTIONED:

IMPACT:

MY "BIG SHINY NEW IDEA" PLAN

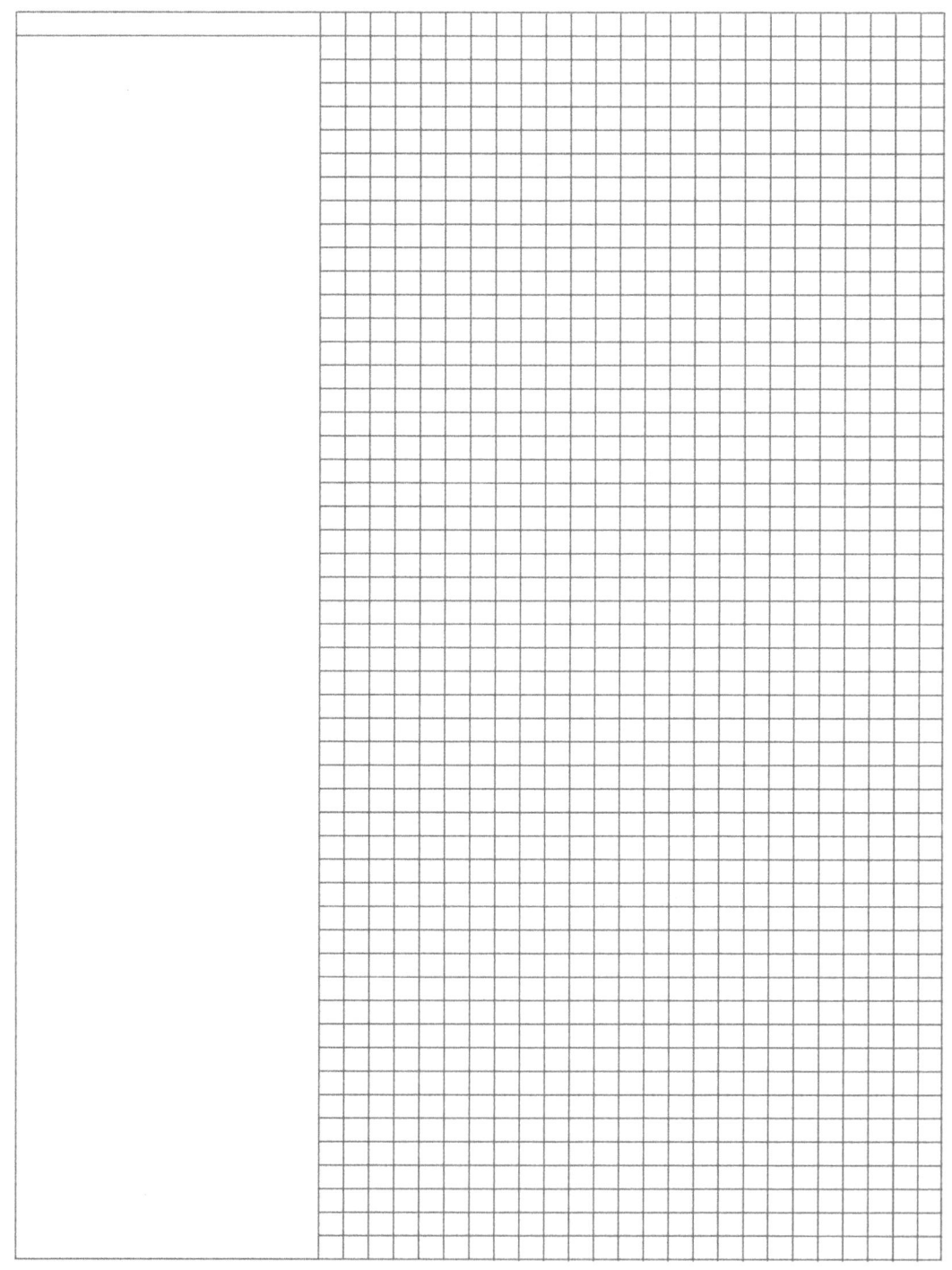

MY "BIG SHINY NEW" IDEA

My idea
....
....
....
....
....
....

> Shine bright my idea. Shine bright.

SENSE CHECK:

☐ Helps with long-term plans
☐ Have the capacity to act
☐ Have the budget to act
☐ Have the skills required

What will make this idea shine?

POTENTIAL IMPACT
1 2 3 4 5 6 7 8 9 10

TIMELINE
NOW   SOON
LATER NEVER

POTENTIAL BENEFITS   **POTENTIAL DRAWBACKS**

ACTIONED: **IMPACT:**

MY "BIG SHINY NEW IDEA" PLAN

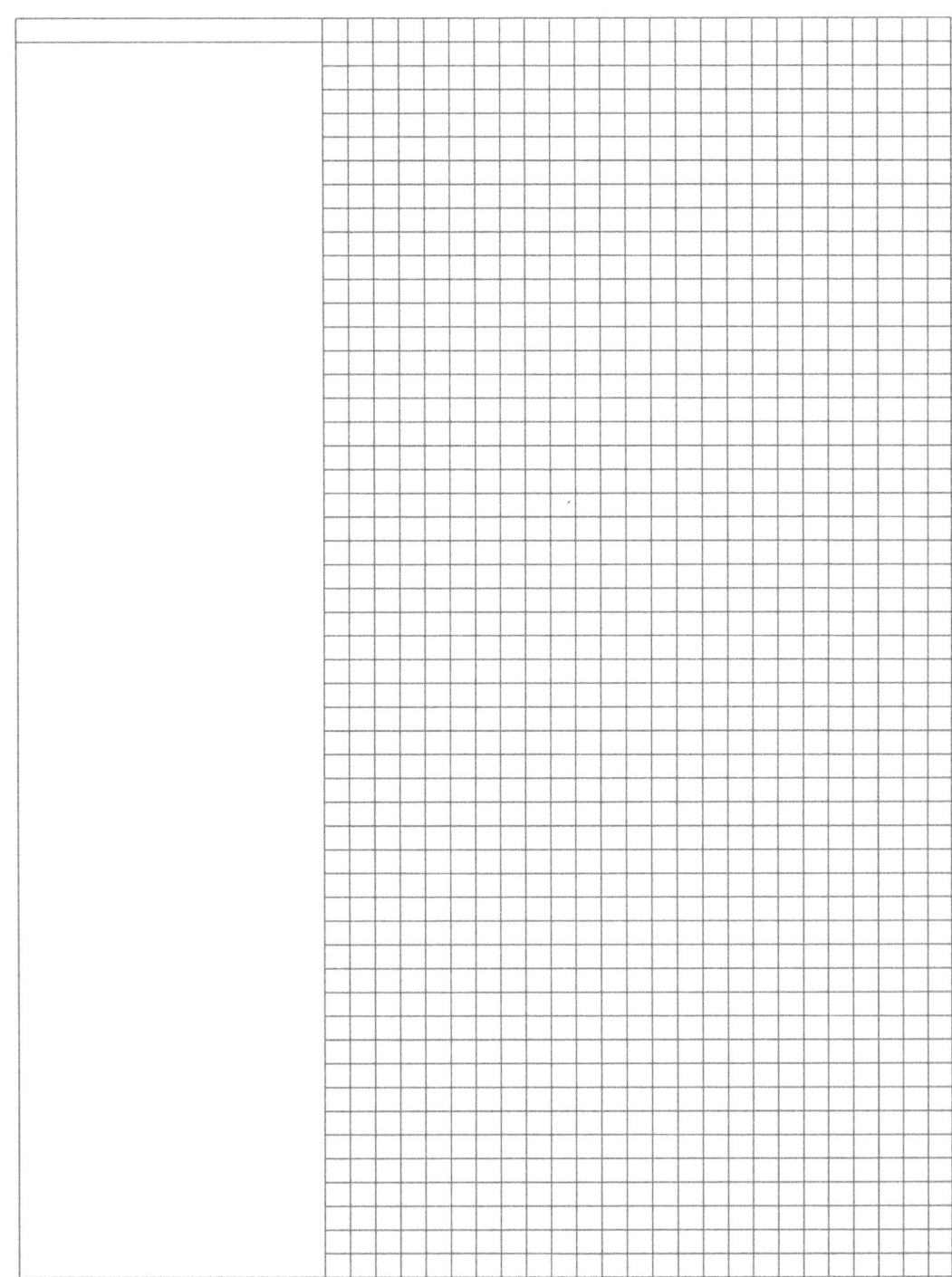

MY "BIG SHINY NEW" IDEA

My idea
....
....
....
....
....

Shine bright my idea. Shine bright.

SENSE CHECK:

☐ Helps with long-term plans
☐ Have the capacity to act
☐ Have the budget to act
☐ Have the skills required

What will make this idea shine?

POTENTIAL IMPACT
1 2 3 4 5 6 7 8 9 10

POTENTIAL BENEFITS   **POTENTIAL DRAWBACKS**

TIMELINE
NOW   SOON
LATER   NEVER

ACTIONED:

IMPACT:

MY "BIG SHINY NEW IDEA" PLAN

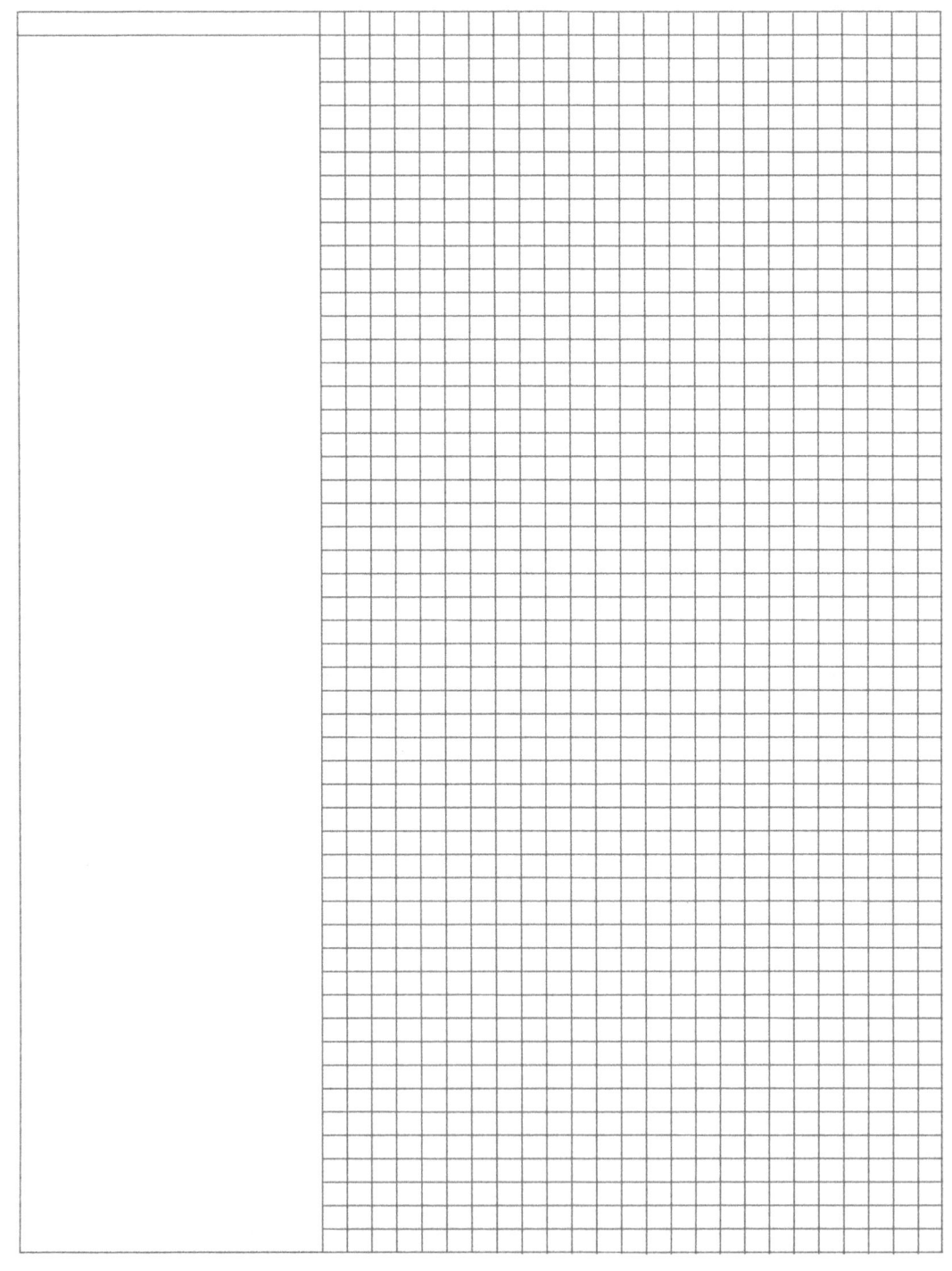

MY "BIG SHINY NEW" IDEA

My idea
....
....
....
....
....
....

Shine bright my idea. Shine bright.

SENSE CHECK:

☐ Helps with long-term plans
☐ Have the capacity to act
☐ Have the budget to act
☐ Have the skills required

What will make this idea shine?

POTENTIAL IMPACT
1 2 3 4 5 6 7 8 9 10

TIMELINE
NOW   SOON
LATER NEVER

POTENTIAL BENEFITS   POTENTIAL DRAWBACKS

ACTIONED:

IMPACT:

MY "BIG SHINY NEW IDEA" PLAN

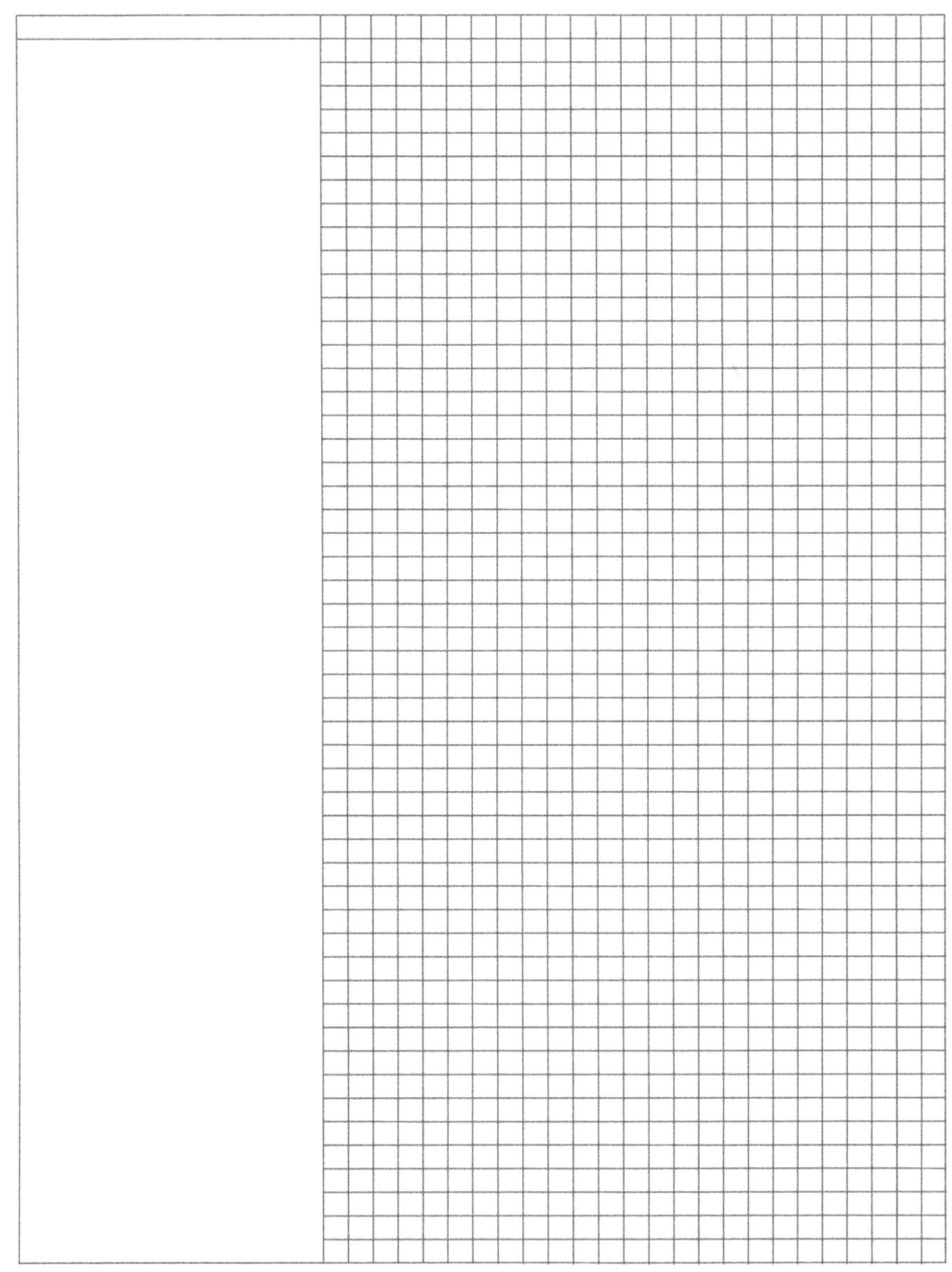

MY "BIG SHINY NEW" IDEA

My idea
....
....
....
....
....
....

Shine bright my idea. Shine bright.

SENSE CHECK:

☐ Helps with long-term plans

☐ Have the capacity to act

☐ Have the budget to act

☐ Have the skills required

What will make this idea shine?

POTENTIAL IMPACT
1 2 3 4 5 6 7 8 9 10

TIMELINE
NOW   SOON
LATER   NEVER

POTENTIAL BENEFITS   POTENTIAL DRAWBACKS

ACTIONED:

IMPACT:

MY "BIG SHINY NEW IDEA" PLAN

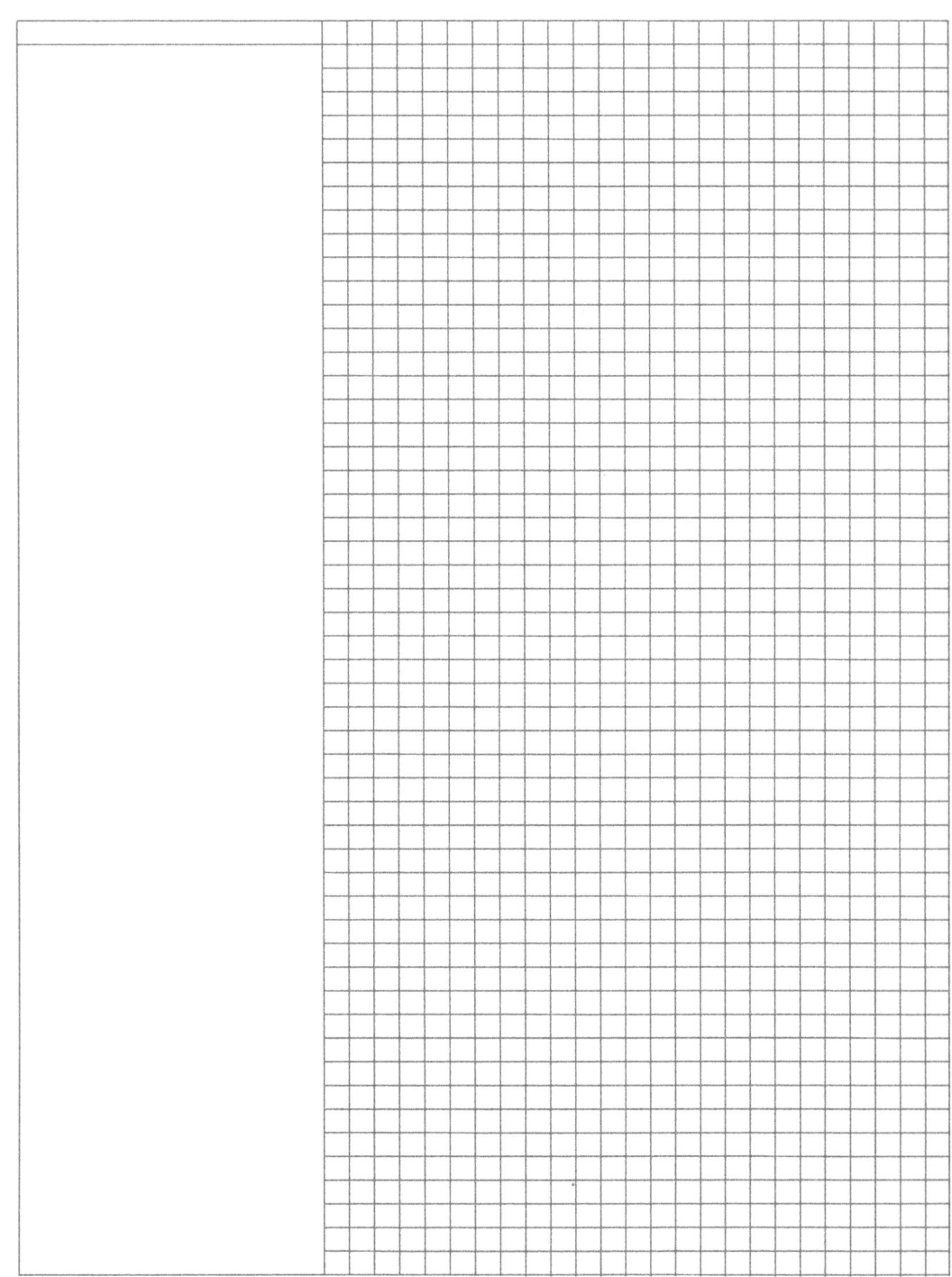

MY "BIG SHINY NEW" IDEA

My idea

....

....

....

....

....

....

Shine bright my idea. Shine bright.

SENSE CHECK:

☐ Helps with long-term plans

☐ Have the capacity to act

☐ Have the budget to act

☐ Have the skills required

What will make this idea shine?

POTENTIAL IMPACT
1 2 3 4 5 6 7 8 9 10

TIMELINE
NOW   SOON
LATER   NEVER

POTENTIAL BENEFITS   POTENTIAL DRAWBACKS

ACTIONED:

IMPACT:

MY "BIG SHINY NEW IDEA" PLAN

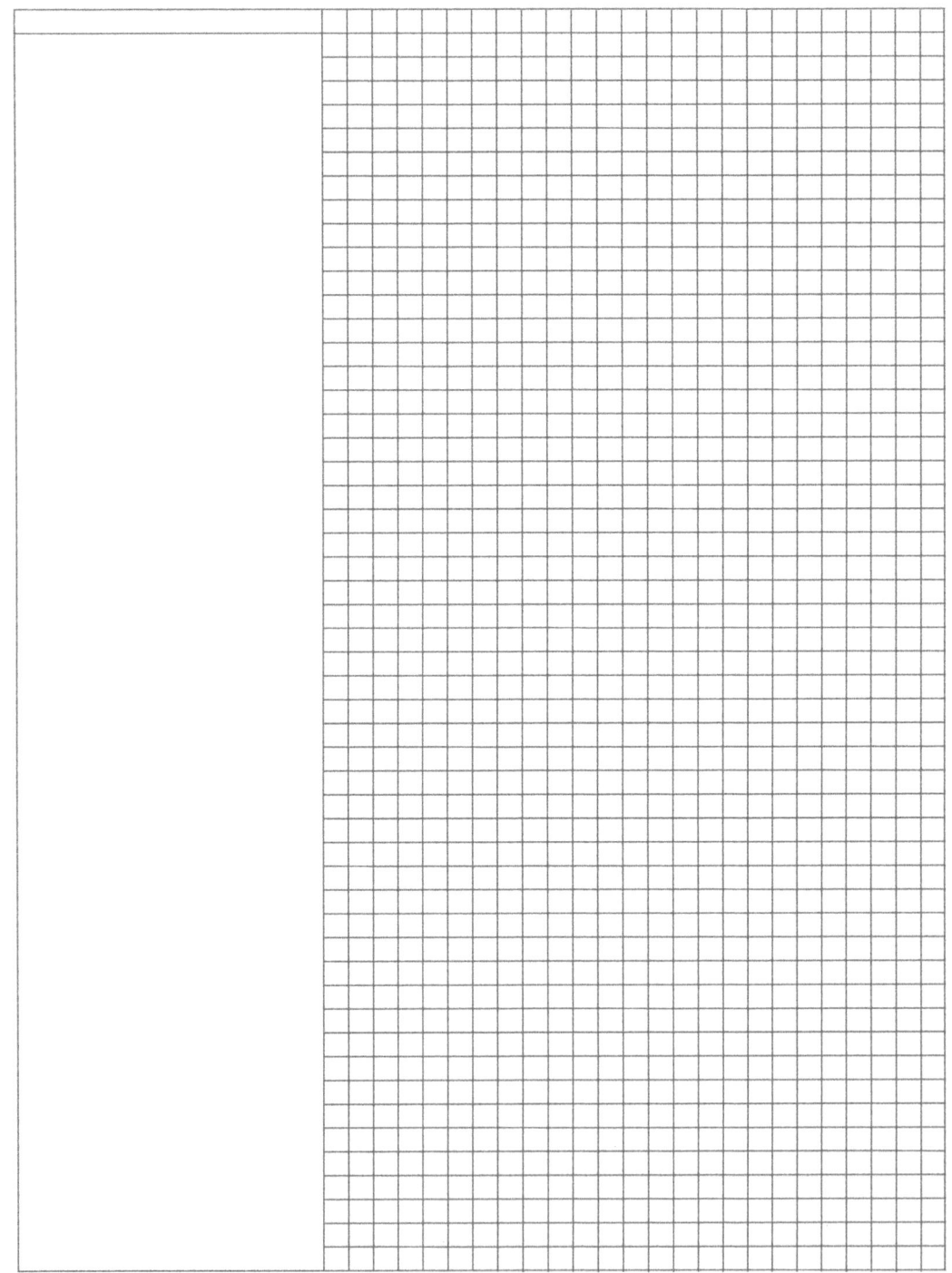

MY "BIG SHINY NEW" IDEA

My idea
....
....
....
....
....
....

Shine bright my idea. Shine bright.

SENSE CHECK:

☐ Helps with long-term plans
☐ Have the capacity to act
☐ Have the budget to act
☐ Have the skills required

What will make this idea shine?

POTENTIAL IMPACT
1 2 3 4 5 6 7 8 9 10

TIMELINE
NOW   SOON
LATER NEVER

POTENTIAL BENEFITS   **POTENTIAL DRAWBACKS**

ACTIONED: **IMPACT:**

MY "BIG SHINY NEW IDEA" PLAN

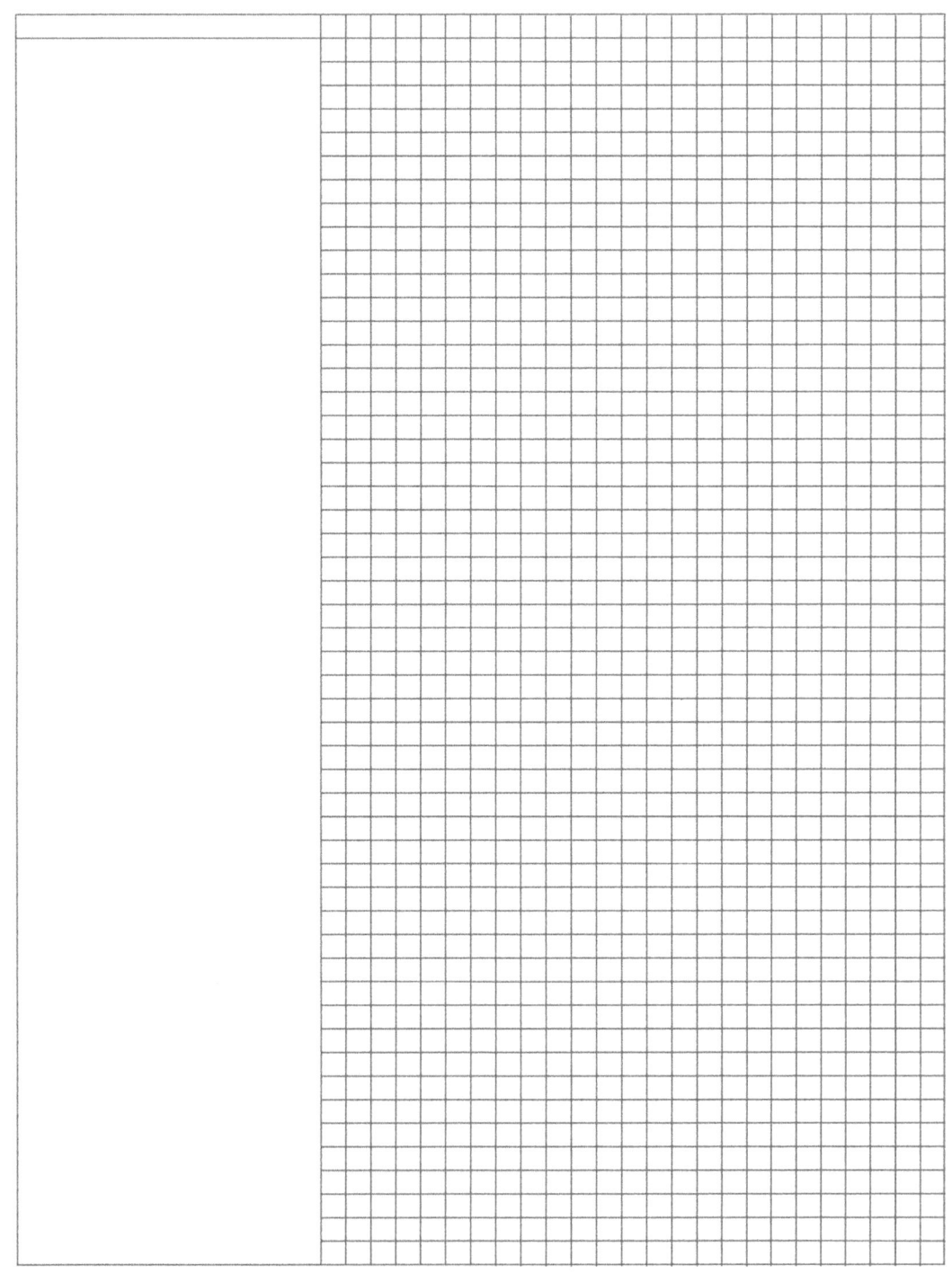

MY "BIG SHINY NEW" IDEA

My idea
....
....
....
....
....

Shine bright my idea. Shine bright.

SENSE CHECK:

☐ Helps with long-term plans
☐ Have the capacity to act
☐ Have the budget to act
☐ Have the skills required

POTENTIAL IMPACT
1 2 3 4 5 6 7 8 9 10

TIMELINE
NOW   SOON
LATER NEVER

What will make this idea shine?

POTENTIAL BENEFITS   POTENTIAL DRAWBACKS

ACTIONED:

IMPACT:

MY "BIG SHINY NEW IDEA" PLAN

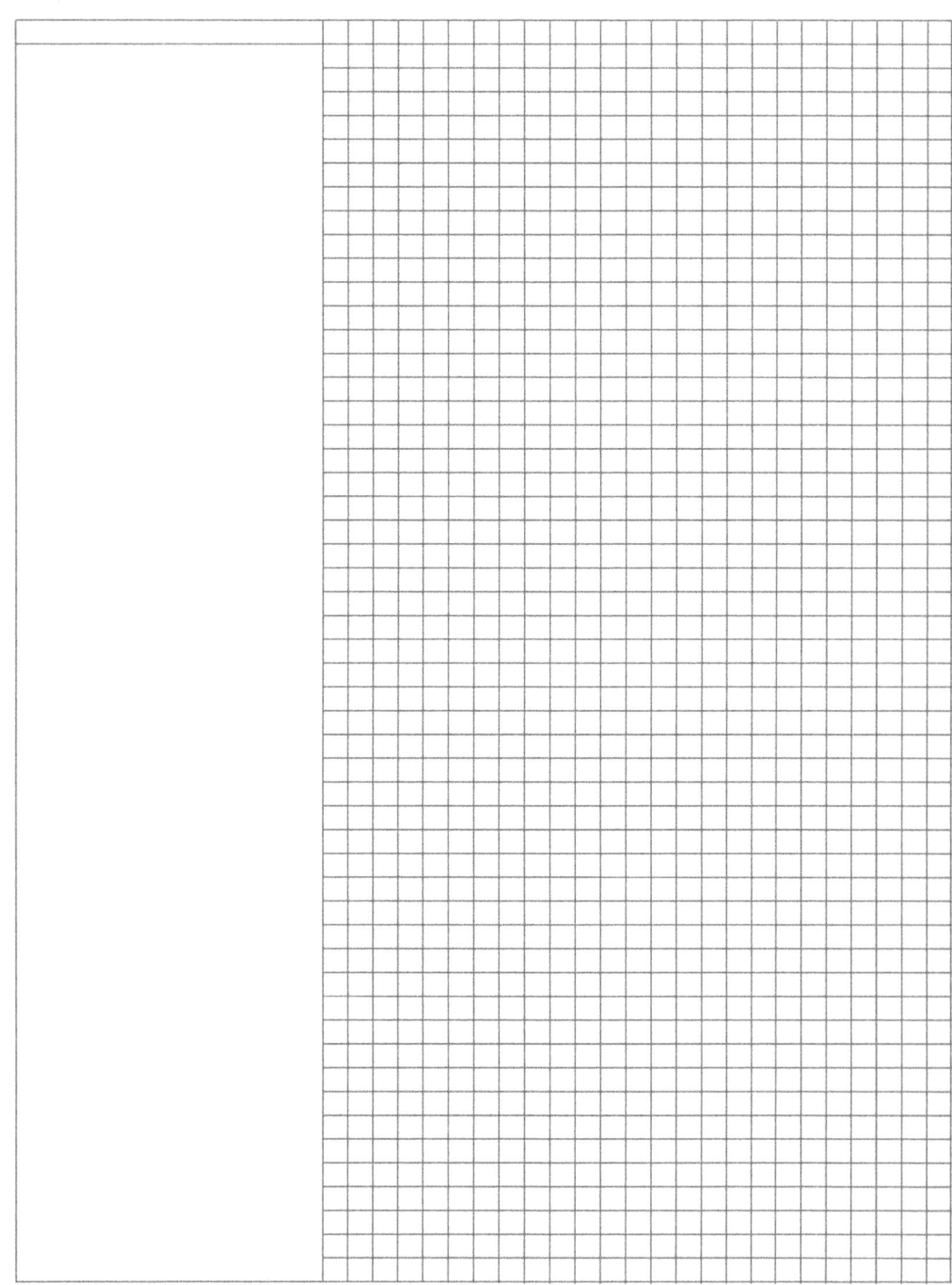

MY "BIG SHINY NEW" IDEA

My idea

....

....

....

....

....

....

Shine bright my idea. Shine bright.

SENSE CHECK:

☐ Helps with long-term plans

☐ Have the capacity to act

☐ Have the budget to act

☐ Have the skills required

What will make this idea shine?

POTENTIAL IMPACT
1 2 3 4 5 6 7 8 9 10

TIMELINE
NOW   SOON
LATER   NEVER

POTENTIAL BENEFITS   POTENTIAL DRAWBACKS

ACTIONED:

IMPACT:

MY "BIG SHINY NEW IDEA" PLAN

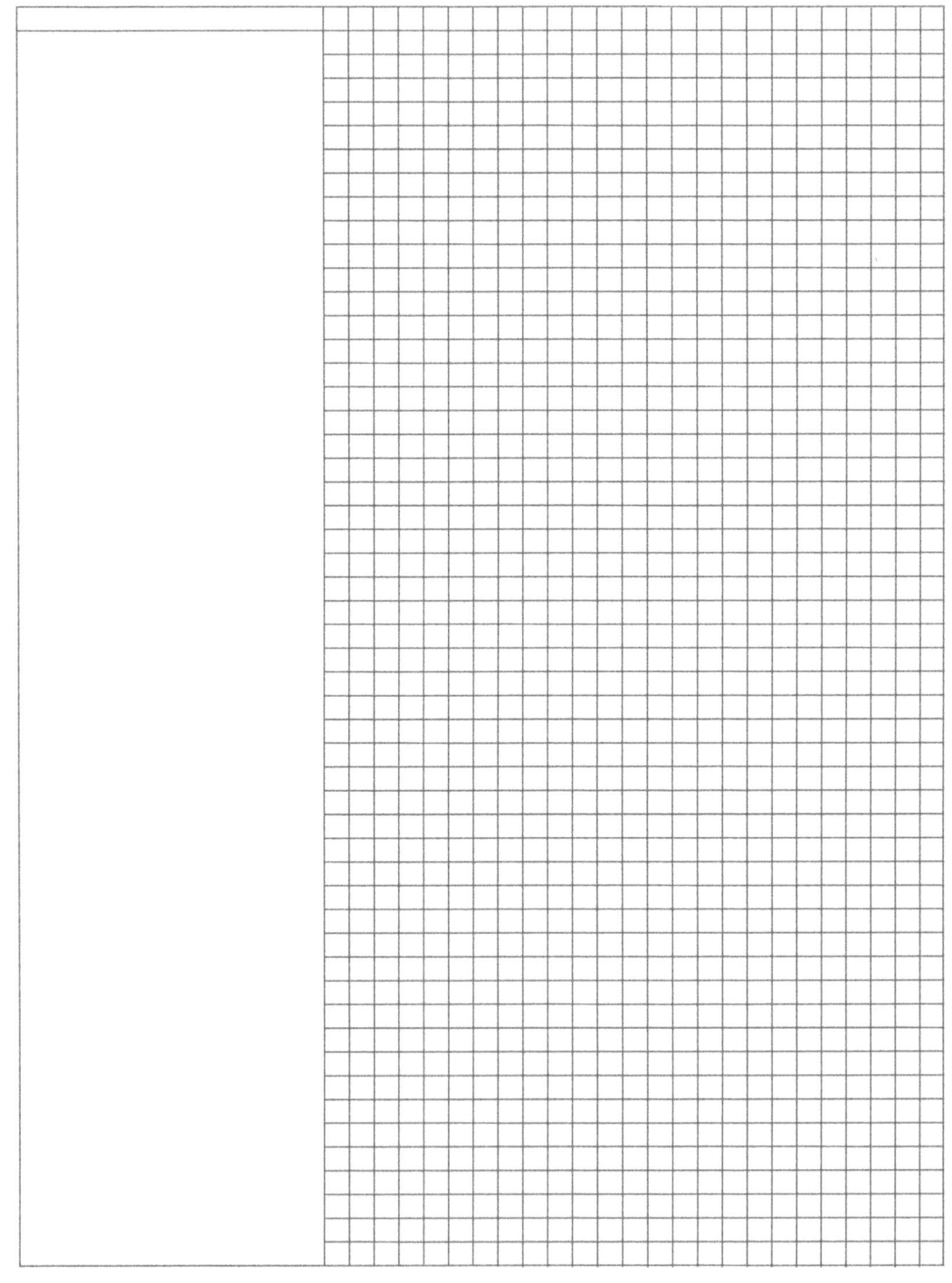

MY "BIG SHINY NEW" IDEA

My idea

....

....

....

....

....

....

> Shine bright my idea. Shine bright.

SENSE CHECK:

☐ Helps with long-term plans

☐ Have the capacity to act

☐ Have the budget to act

☐ Have the skills required

What will make this idea shine?

POTENTIAL IMPACT
1 2 3 4 5 6 7 8 9 10

POTENTIAL BENEFITS   **POTENTIAL DRAWBACKS**

TIMELINE
NOW   SOON
LATER NEVER

ACTIONED:

IMPACT:

MY "BIG SHINY NEW IDEA" PLAN

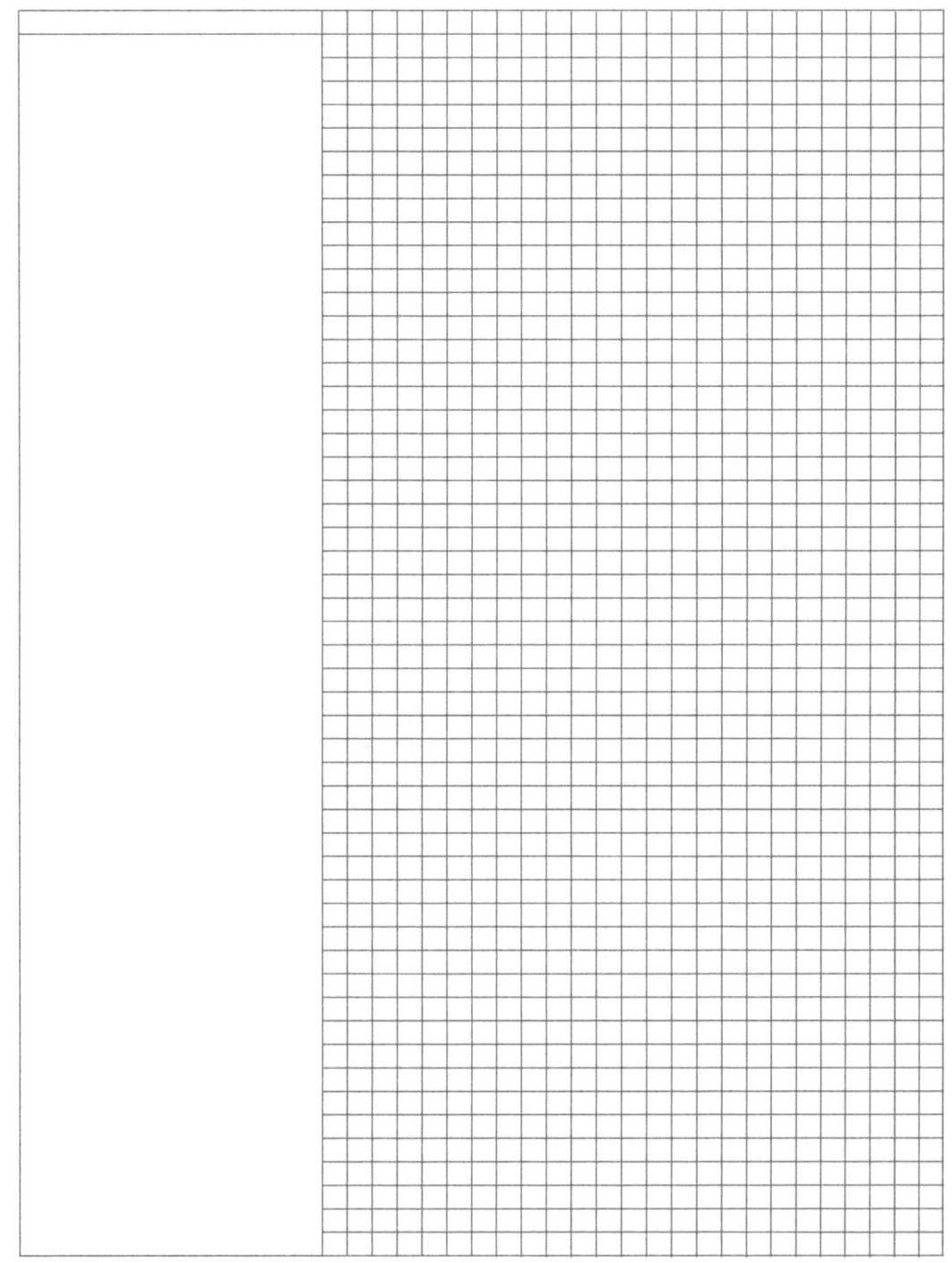

MY "BIG SHINY NEW" IDEA

My idea

....
....
....
....
....
....

Shine bright my idea. Shine bright.

SENSE CHECK:

☐ Helps with long-term plans

☐ Have the capacity to act

☐ Have the budget to act

☐ Have the skills required

What will make this idea shine?

POTENTIAL IMPACT
1 2 3 4 5 6 7 8 9 10

TIMELINE
NOW   SOON
LATER   NEVER

POTENTIAL BENEFITS   POTENTIAL DRAWBACKS

ACTIONED:

IMPACT:

MY "BIG SHINY NEW IDEA" PLAN

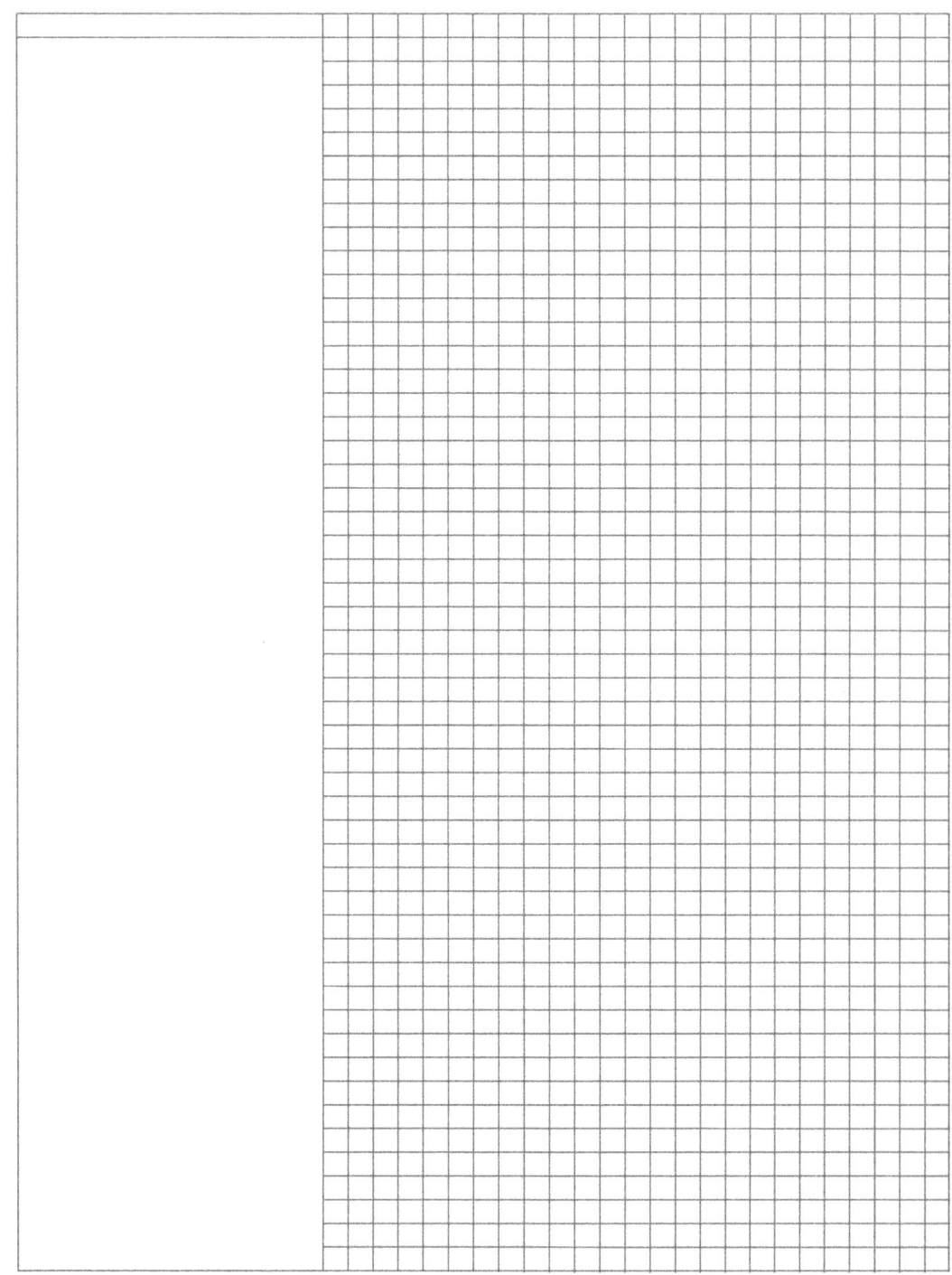

MY "BIG SHINY NEW" IDEA

My idea

....

....

....

....

....

....

Shine bright my idea. Shine bright.

SENSE CHECK:

☐ Helps with long-term plans

☐ Have the capacity to act

☐ Have the budget to act

☐ Have the skills required

What will make this idea shine?

POTENTIAL IMPACT
1 2 3 4 5 6 7 8 9 10

POTENTIAL BENEFITS   **POTENTIAL DRAWBACKS**

TIMELINE
NOW   SOON
LATER   NEVER

ACTIONED:

IMPACT:

MY "BIG SHINY NEW IDEA" PLAN

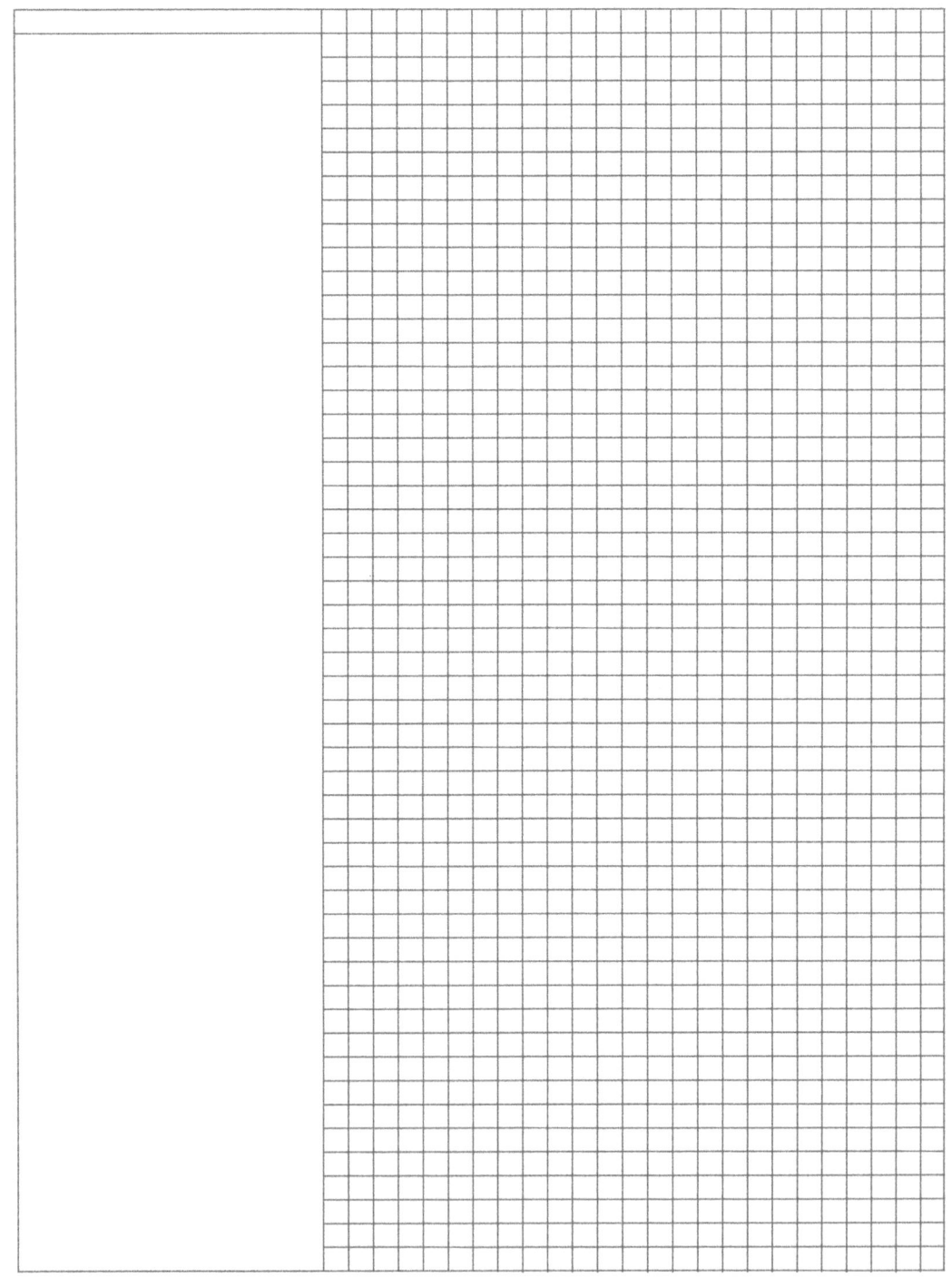

MY "BIG SHINY NEW" IDEA

My idea

....

....

....

....

....

Shine bright my idea. Shine bright.

SENSE CHECK:

☐ Helps with long-term plans

☐ Have the capacity to act

☐ Have the budget to act

☐ Have the skills required

What will make this idea shine?

POTENTIAL IMPACT
1 2 3 4 5 6 7 8 9 10

TIMELINE
NOW   SOON
LATER NEVER

POTENTIAL BENEFITS   POTENTIAL DRAWBACKS

ACTIONED:

IMPACT:

MY "BIG SHINY NEW IDEA" PLAN

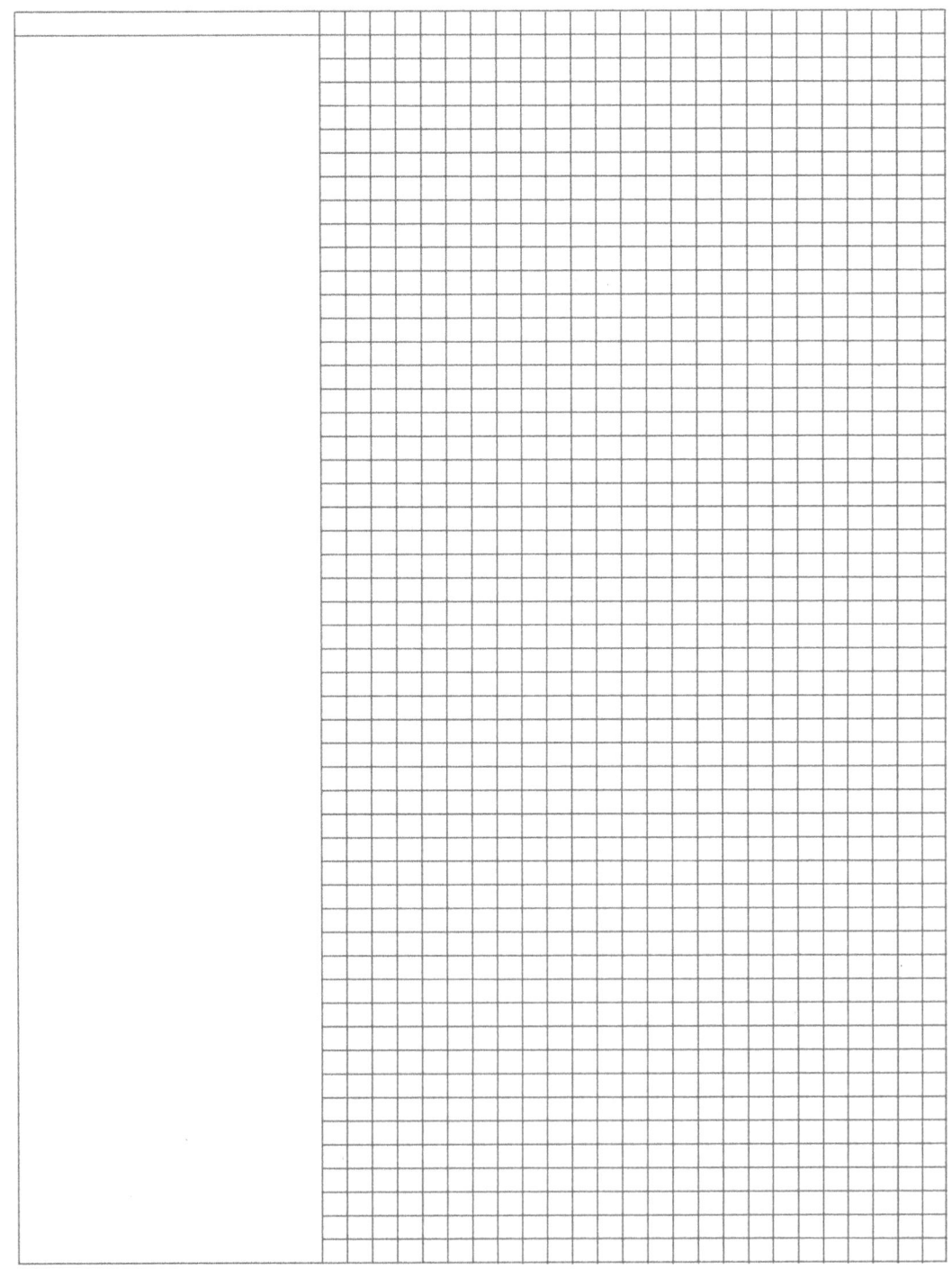

MY "BIG SHINY NEW" IDEA

My idea

....

....

....

....

....

....

> Shine bright my idea. Shine bright.

SENSE CHECK:

- [ ] Helps with long-term plans
- [ ] Have the capacity to act
- [ ] Have the budget to act
- [ ] Have the skills required

What will make this idea shine?

POTENTIAL IMPACT
1 2 3 4 5 6 7 8 9 10

TIMELINE
NOW   SOON
LATER NEVER

POTENTIAL BENEFITS	POTENTIAL DRAWBACKS

ACTIONED:

IMPACT:

MY "BIG SHINY NEW IDEA" PLAN

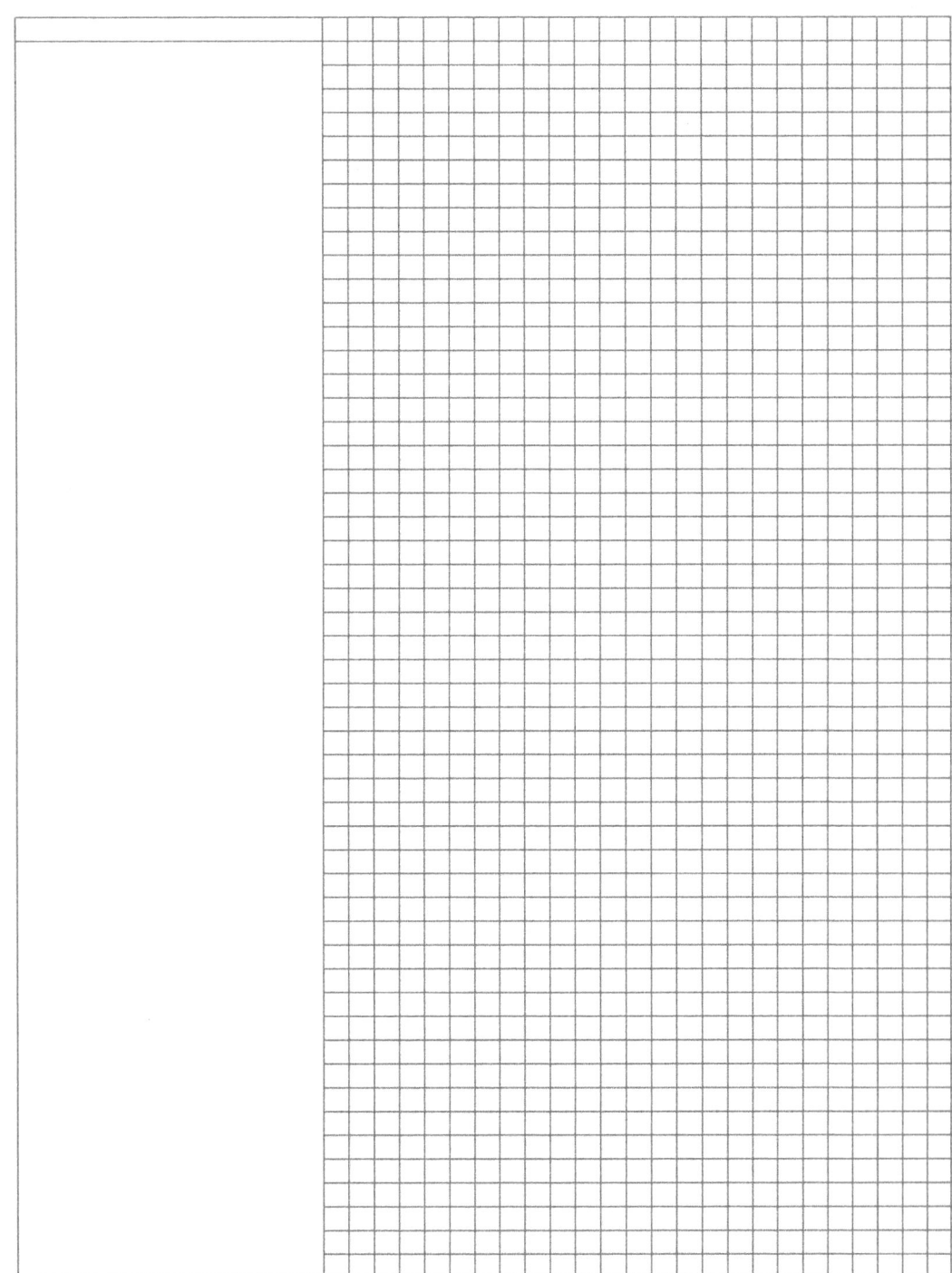

MY "BIG SHINY NEW" IDEA

My idea

....

....

....

....

....

....

Shine bright my idea. Shine bright.

SENSE CHECK:

☐ Helps with long-term plans

☐ Have the capacity to act

☐ Have the budget to act

☐ Have the skills required

What will make this idea shine?

POTENTIAL IMPACT
1 2 3 4 5 6 7 8 9 10

TIMELINE
NOW   SOON
LATER   NEVER

POTENTIAL BENEFITS   POTENTIAL DRAWBACKS

ACTIONED:

IMPACT:

MY "BIG SHINY NEW IDEA" PLAN

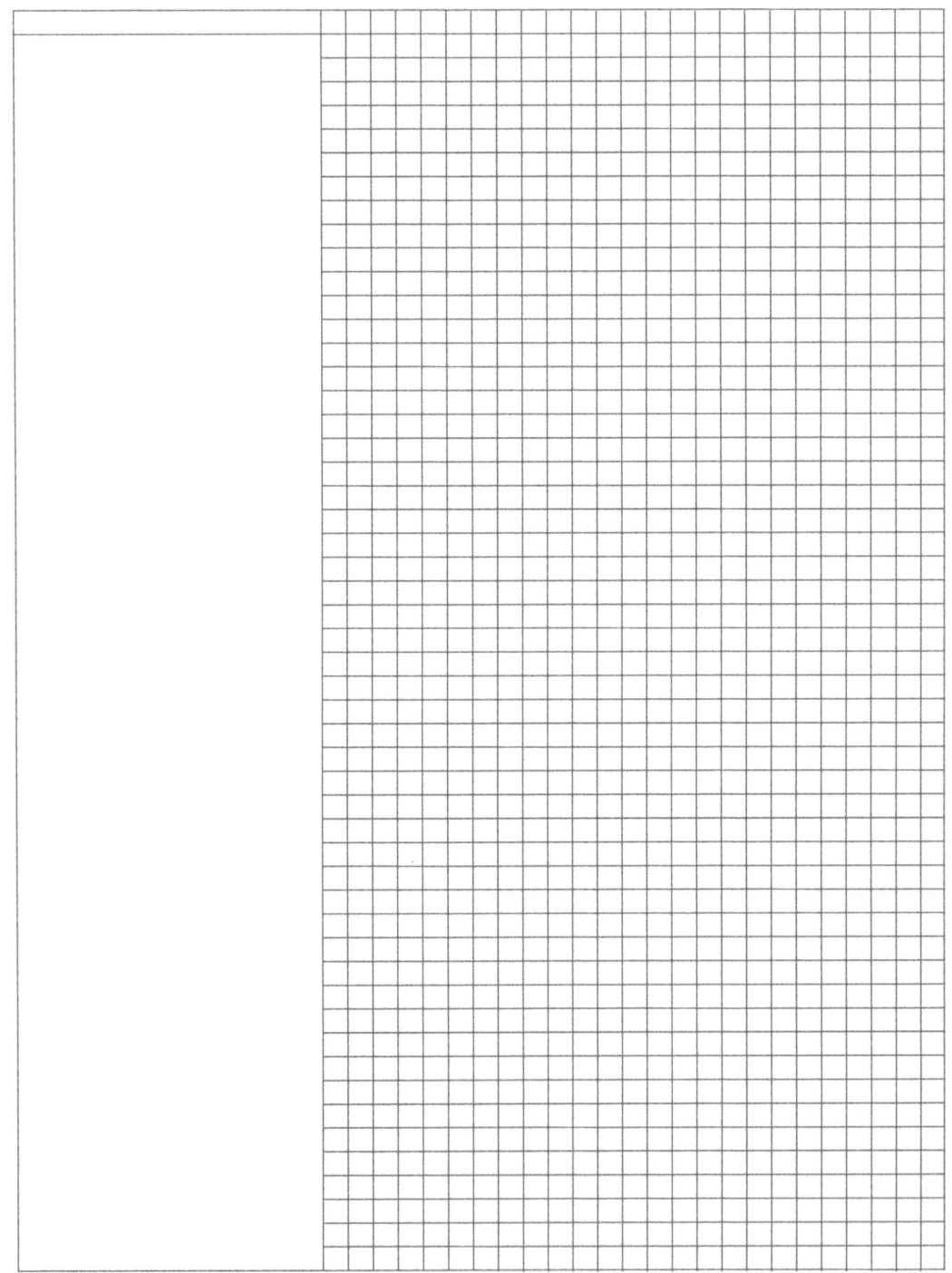

MY "BIG SHINY NEW" IDEA

My idea
....
....
....
....
....
....

Shine bright my idea. Shine bright.

SENSE CHECK:

☐ Helps with long-term plans
☐ Have the capacity to act
☐ Have the budget to act
☐ Have the skills required

What will make this idea shine?

POTENTIAL IMPACT
1 2 3 4 5 6 7 8 9 10

TIMELINE
NOW   SOON
LATER NEVER

POTENTIAL BENEFITS   POTENTIAL DRAWBACKS

ACTIONED:

IMPACT:

MY "BIG SHINY NEW IDEA" PLAN

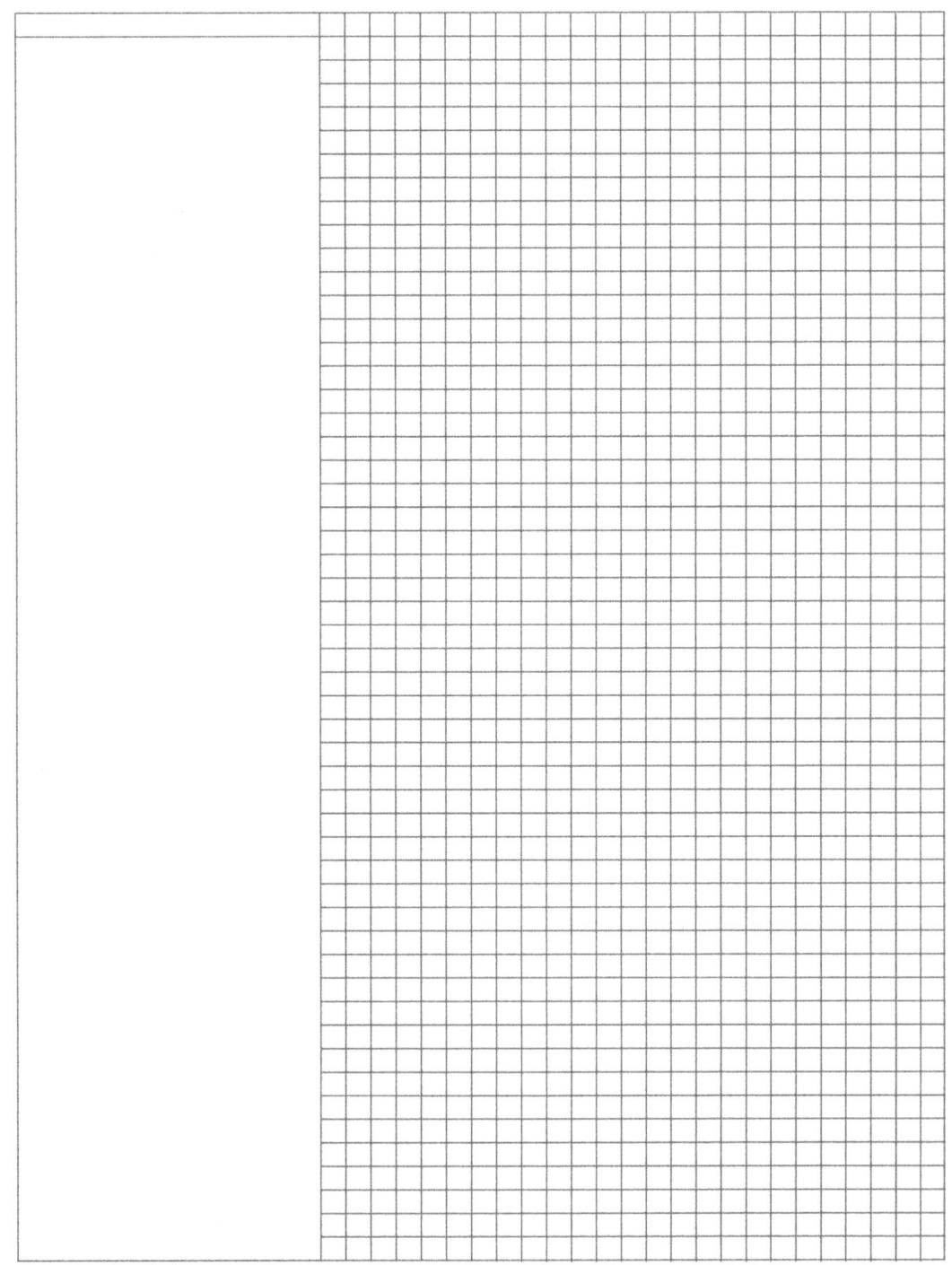

MY "BIG SHINY NEW" IDEA

My idea
....
....
....
....
....
....

Shine bright my idea. Shine bright.

SENSE CHECK:

☐ Helps with long-term plans

☐ Have the capacity to act

☐ Have the budget to act

☐ Have the skills required

POTENTIAL IMPACT
1 2 3 4 5 6 7 8 9 10

TIMELINE
NOW   SOON
LATER   NEVER

What will make this idea shine?

POTENTIAL BENEFITS   **POTENTIAL DRAWBACKS**

ACTIONED: **IMPACT:**

MY "BIG SHINY NEW IDEA" PLAN

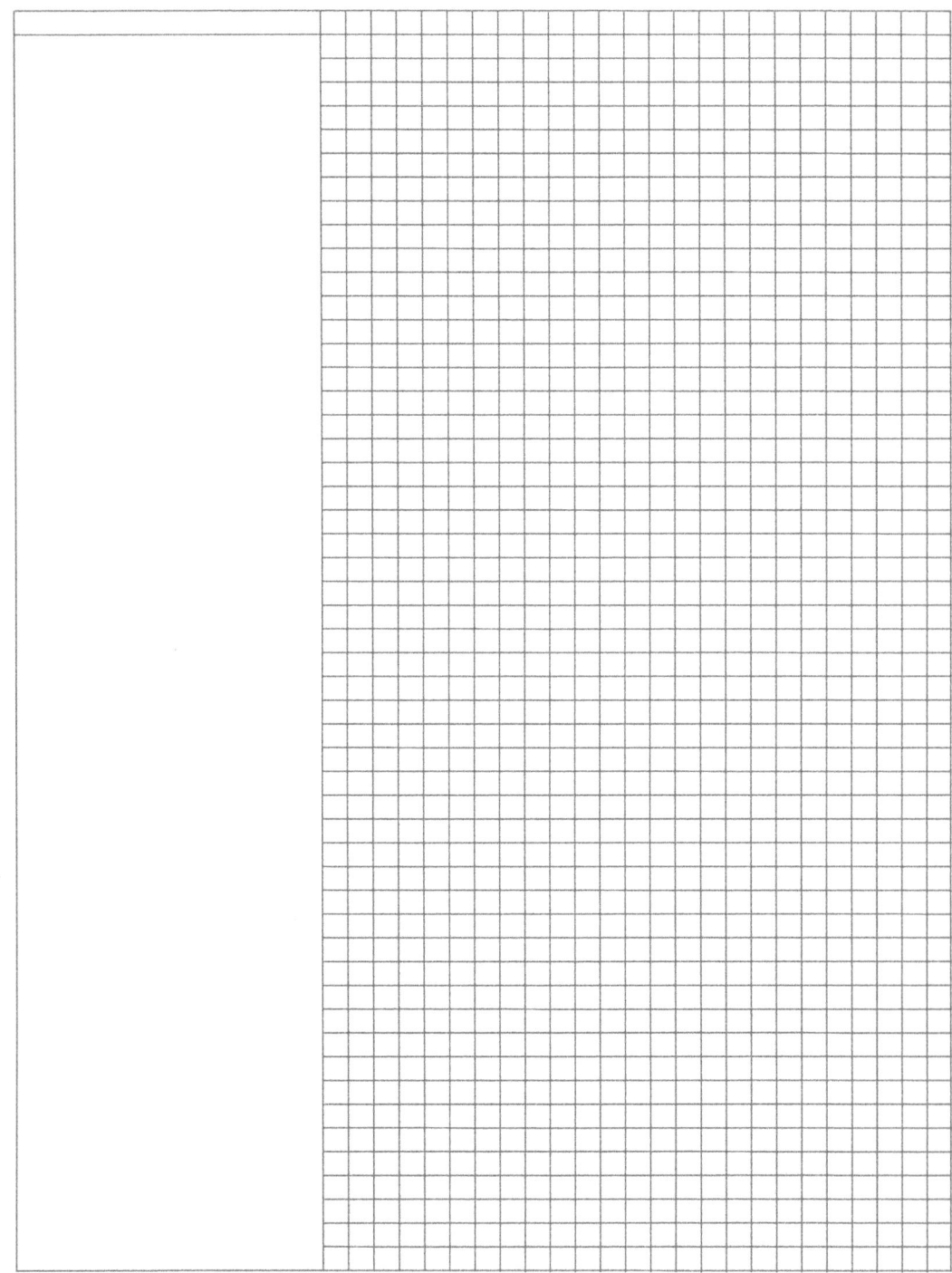

MY "BIG SHINY NEW" IDEA

My idea

....

....

....

....

....

....

Shine bright my idea. Shine bright.

SENSE CHECK:

☐ Helps with long-term plans

☐ Have the capacity to act

☐ Have the budget to act

☐ Have the skills required

What will make this idea shine?

POTENTIAL IMPACT
1 2 3 4 5 6 7 8 9 10

TIMELINE
NOW   SOON
LATER NEVER

POTENTIAL BENEFITS   POTENTIAL DRAWBACKS

ACTIONED:

IMPACT:

MY "BIG SHINY NEW IDEA" PLAN

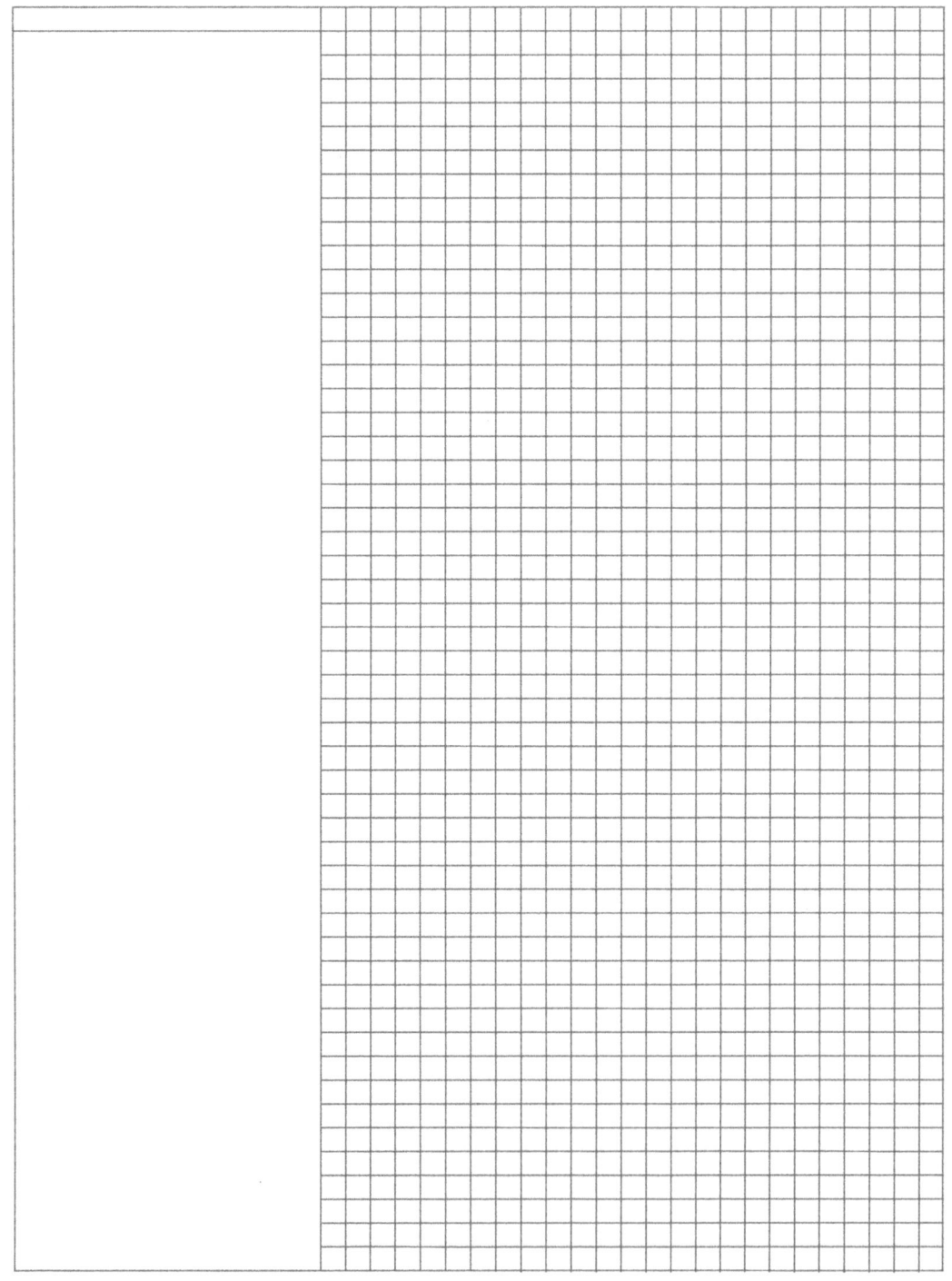

MY "BIG SHINY NEW" IDEA

My idea

....

....

....

....

....

Shine bright my idea. Shine bright.

SENSE CHECK:

☐ Helps with long-term plans

☐ Have the capacity to act

☐ Have the budget to act

☐ Have the skills required

What will make this idea shine?

POTENTIAL IMPACT
1 2 3 4 5 6 7 8 9 10

POTENTIAL BENEFITS   **POTENTIAL DRAWBACKS**

TIMELINE
NOW   SOON
LATER   NEVER

ACTIONED:

IMPACT:

MY "BIG SHINY NEW IDEA" PLAN

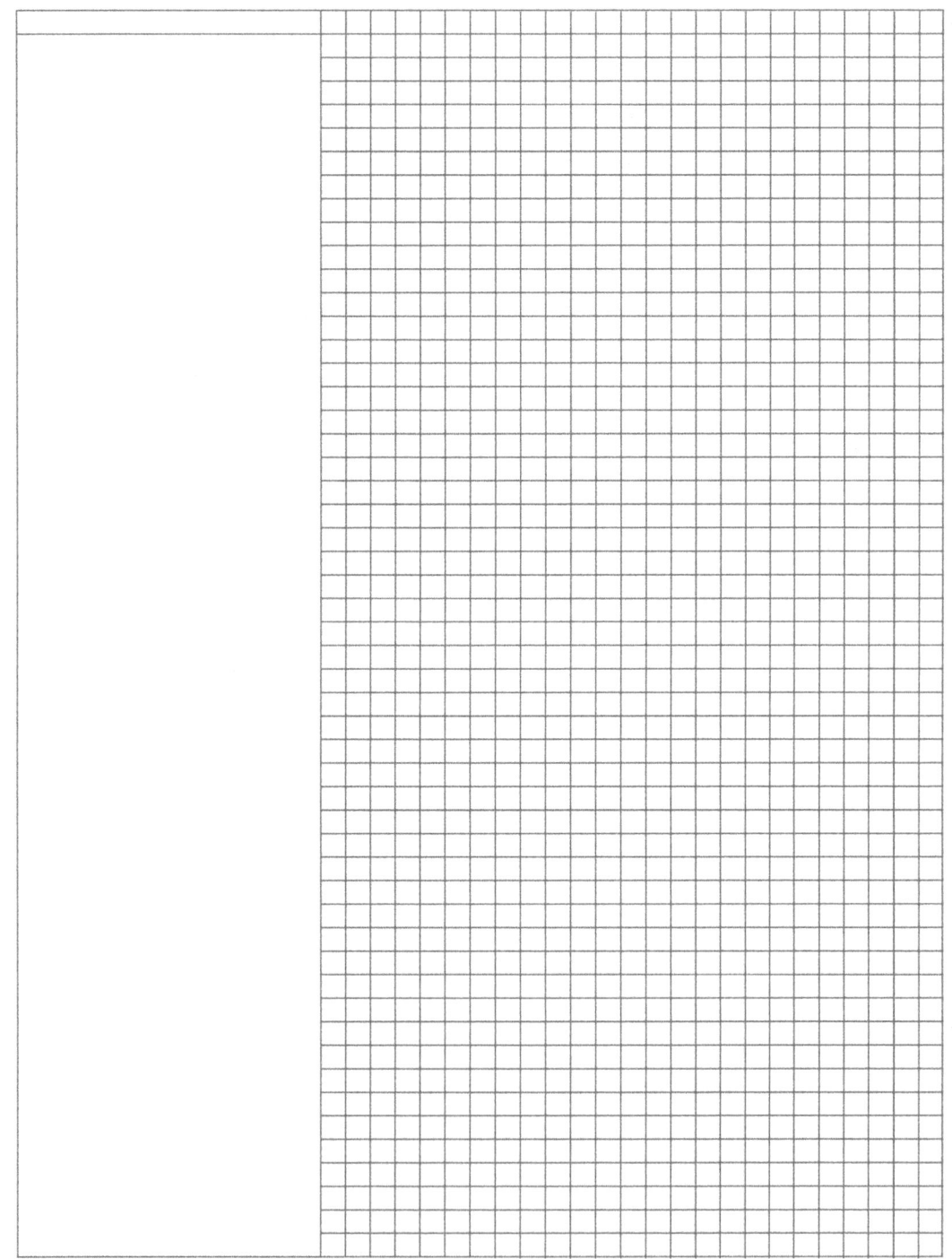

MY "BIG SHINY NEW" IDEA

My idea

....

....

....

....

....

....

Shine bright my idea. Shine bright.

SENSE CHECK:

☐ Helps with long-term plans

☐ Have the capacity to act

☐ Have the budget to act

☐ Have the skills required

POTENTIAL IMPACT
1 2 3 4 5 6 7 8 9 10

TIMELINE
NOW   SOON
LATER   NEVER

What will make this idea shine?

POTENTIAL BENEFITS   **POTENTIAL DRAWBACKS**

ACTIONED:

IMPACT:

MY "BIG SHINY NEW IDEA" PLAN

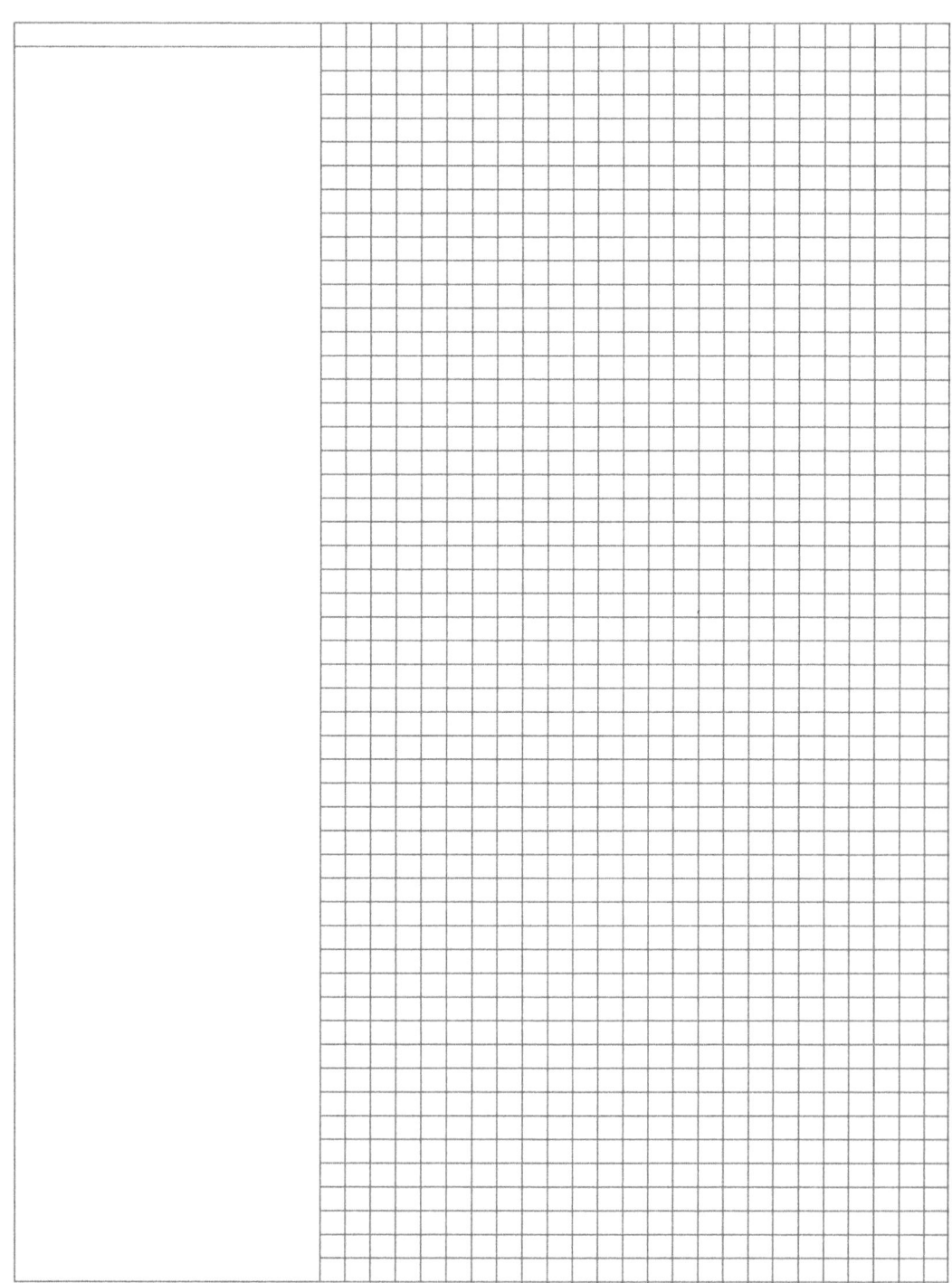

MY "BIG SHINY NEW" IDEA

My idea

....

....

....

....

....

....

Shine bright my idea. Shine bright.

SENSE CHECK:

☐ Helps with long-term plans

☐ Have the capacity to act

☐ Have the budget to act

☐ Have the skills required

What will make this idea shine?

POTENTIAL IMPACT
1 2 3 4 5 6 7 8 9 10

TIMELINE
NOW   SOON
LATER   NEVER

POTENTIAL BENEFITS   POTENTIAL DRAWBACKS

ACTIONED:

IMPACT:

MY "BIG SHINY NEW IDEA" PLAN

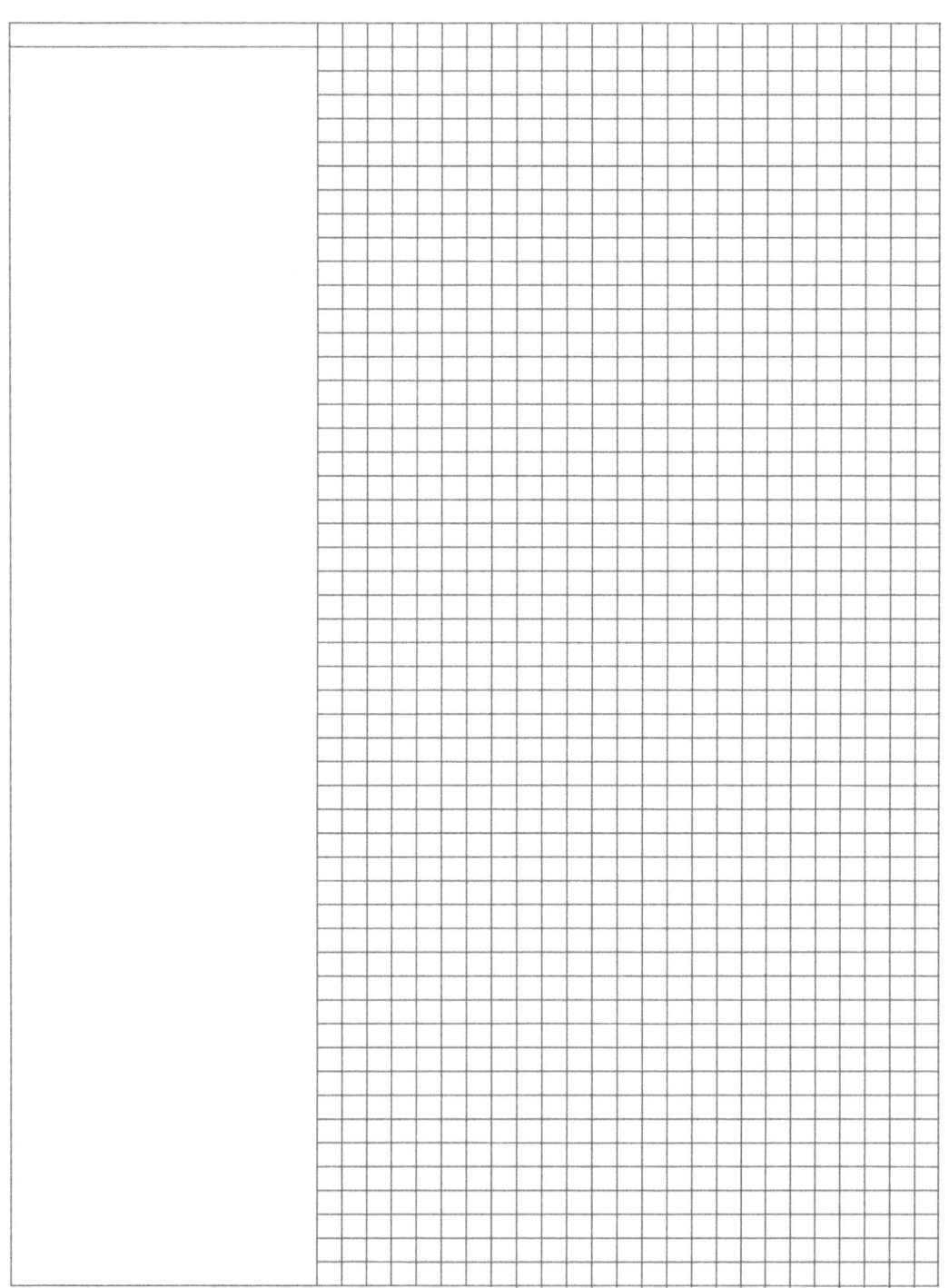

MY "BIG SHINY NEW" IDEA

My idea

....

....

....

....

....

Shine bright my idea. Shine bright.

SENSE CHECK:

- ☐ Helps with long-term plans
- ☐ Have the capacity to act
- ☐ Have the budget to act
- ☐ Have the skills required

POTENTIAL IMPACT
1 2 3 4 5 6 7 8 9 10

TIMELINE
NOW   SOON
LATER NEVER

What will make this idea shine?

POTENTIAL BENEFITS   POTENTIAL DRAWBACKS

ACTIONED:

IMPACT:

MY "BIG SHINY NEW IDEA" PLAN

TO DO LIST

- Map it out in here
- Create the content needed for the info pages
- Brief Jane
- Work using the same templates as last time.
- Create teaser videos to build interest.
- Load up for printers
- Create imagery for Shopify and Amazon
- Create TIKTOKS, stories and send email to list
- Add to FB Ad set once stock in

What else could I make?

Why am I doing this?

(check the ego Check

- am I happy with everything else I'm doing?

Why do I need to do this?

We all ok?)

I REALLY LIKE THIS IDEA

MY "BIG SHINY NEW" IDEA

My idea

Create a journal for other people like me who are easily distracted by shiny object syndrome

Shine bright my idea. Shine bright.

SENSE CHECK:

 Helps with long-term plans

 Have the capacity to act

 Have the budget to act

☐ Have the skills required

POTENTIAL IMPACT

1 2 3 4 5 6 7 8 9 10

TIMELINE
NOW   SOON
LATER   NEVER

What will make this idea shine?

- I will need Jane to help with design
- This means I'll be able to link to the journal meta doesn't like the name of
- I'll need to make a case with the CFO
- I'll give it as a gift to clients

POTENTIAL BENEFITS
- gift for clients
- good add on to my book
- builds my brand
- attracts other ND people like me
- Broadens the product range

POTENTIAL DRAWBACKS
- Could distract from our core offers
- Need to be firm about my time in this - and the cost to design up
- Ordering too many and having too much stock on hand

ACTIONED:

IMPACT:

YOUR "BIG SHINY IDEAS JOURNAL" CREATOR
~ Rachel Klaver ~

Distraction is one of my secret weapons. I love allowing myself to follow my nose, explore, discover. It helps my business and my client.
BUT - It can also be extremely dangerous too.

Sometimes my amazing idea is really me trying to avoid an activity that's really going to positively impact my business.

Sometimes it's going to drop my gaze from what really counts.

I believe us ideas people need to celebrate our ideas. We need to give them room and space to see if they're worth pursuing. And we also need to be brave enough to let them stay an idea if we need to.

This journal came from another idea I had rolling around in my head for a while. I used the same principles here to pop it into the "later" pile while I focussed on higher-priority tasks.

But I knew I was coming back for it.
And now here we are!

Here's to us, and to our **BIG NEW SHINY IDEAS**.
Long may we have them, explore them and use the best ones.

~ *Rachel*

Concept created and designed: Rachel Klaver
Layout and cover design: Jane Dang
Editing: Rebekah Potter

www.ingramcontent.com/pod-product-compliance
Lightning Source LLC
Chambersburg PA
CBHW062041290426
44109CB00026B/2693